CAMBRIDGE LIBRARY COLLECTION

Books of enduring scholarly value

East and South-East Asian History

This series focuses on East and South-East Asia from the early modern period to the end of the Victorian era. It includes contemporary accounts of European encounters with the civilisations of China, Japan and South-East Asia from the time of the Jesuit missions and the East India companies to the Chinese revolution of 1911.

Address to the People of Great Britain, Explanatory of Our Commercial Relations with the Empire of China

This anonymous work, sometimes attributed to G.J. Gordon, a researcher into tea cultivation, was published in 1836 after the East India Company's loss of its monopoly on trade two years earlier had opened up the market to private individuals. The pamphlet is aimed at a popular readership and feeds national anxiety about the British government's weak stance towards China and potential trade. It outlines the history and characteristics of the country and its society, and the reasons why previously stifled trade should now flourish. Based on first-hand knowledge, the work is observant and insightful, yet zealous and inflammatory in its tone. Convinced that British goods are equal or superior to Chinese products, the author exhorts the British government to take a firm hand and demand the respect of the Chinese people and their 'insolent' rulers in order to tap into the potentially huge free-trade market.

T0345385

Cambridge University Press has long been a pioneer in the reissuing of out-of-print titles from its own backlist, producing digital reprints of books that are still sought after by scholars and students but could not be reprinted economically using traditional technology. The Cambridge Library Collection extends this activity to a wider range of books which are still of importance to researchers and professionals, either for the source material they contain, or as landmarks in the history of their academic discipline.

Drawing from the world-renowned collections in the Cambridge University Library and other partner libraries, and guided by the advice of experts in each subject area, Cambridge University Press is using state-of-the-art scanning machines in its own Printing House to capture the content of each book selected for inclusion. The files are processed to give a consistently clear, crisp image, and the books finished to the high quality standard for which the Press is recognised around the world. The latest print-on-demand technology ensures that the books will remain available indefinitely, and that orders for single or multiple copies can quickly be supplied.

The Cambridge Library Collection brings back to life books of enduring scholarly value (including out-of-copyright works originally issued by other publishers) across a wide range of disciplines in the humanities and social sciences and in science and technology.

Address to the People of Great Britain,

Explanatory of Our Commercial Relations with the Empire of China

ANONYMOUS

CAMBRIDGE UNIVERSITY PRESS

Cambridge, New York, Melbourne, Madrid, Cape Town,
Singapore, São Paolo, Delhi, Mexico City

Published in the United States of America by Cambridge University Press, New York

www.cambridge.org
Information on this title: www.cambridge.org/9781108045568

© in this compilation Cambridge University Press 2013

This edition first published 1836
This digitally printed version 2013

ISBN 978-1-108-04556-8 Paperback

ADDRESS

TO THE

PEOPLE OF GREAT BRITAIN,

EXPLANATORY OF

OUR COMMERCIAL RELATIONS WITH THE

EMPIRE OF CHINA,

AND OF

THE COURSE OF POLICY BY WHICH IT MAY BE RENDERED

AN ALMOST UNBOUNDED FIELD FOR

BRITISH COMMERCE.

———————

BY A VISITOR TO CHINA.

———————

LONDON:

SMITH, ELDER AND CO., CORNHILL,

BOOKSELLERS TO THEIR MAJESTIES.

1836.

LONDON :
PRINTED BY STEWART AND CO.
OLD BAILEY.

ADVERTISEMENT.

It is proper to premise, that this attempt to throw light on a subject which has been much misrepresented, and is but little understood by the public at large, is from the pen of a gentleman who visited China for purposes entirely unconnected with commerce; and who, with the advantage of personal observation, may reasonably be supposed to have formed a more impartial and dispassionate judgment, than could have been arrived at by one writing under the smart of the injuries which he portrays.

ADDRESS,

CHINA, exclusive of its possessions in Tartary, which spread over seventy degrees of longitude, comprises, within the circuit of its proper territories, a superficies of nearly one million three hundred thousand square miles, or upwards of ten times the computed area of the British isles.

Nor is the vastness of this empire to be estimated merely by the space over which it spreads, since in point of extent, China Proper yields to the Russian empire, which stretches from the shores of the Baltic to the sea of Kamtschatka, and from the Caspian to the Polar ocean. In the number of its inhabitants, however, it surpasses Russia and all other countries.

The immensity of its population indeed, as reported in the official returns made to government, may well stagger belief; but the correctness of those statements need not here be made a subject of disquisition. Suffice it to observe, that we have the concurrent testimony of almost all travellers, from the time of Marco Polo to the present hour, that the number of cities, towns, and villages, great as it is

B

in all the provinces, is, in many, almost inconceivable.

The report made to Sir George Staunton, states the population to be three hundred and thirty-three millions; nearly one-third of the number of human beings supposed to exist over the whole face of the globe. In fact, we have no record of the existence of a country so densely populated, subject to one government, using one language, and observing one system of laws and institutions.

Nor does the population, as under some other despotisms, consist of only two classes, the lordly and wealthy tyrant, and the wretched slave. There is in China every gradation of society that is met with in Europe; and, though there are certain privileges exclusively pertaining to the members of the Imperial family and the functionaries of government, wealth is distributed also among the private gentry, as well as among a very numerous and enterprising mercantile community; nor are the manufacturers and artisans denied the reward of ingenuity and industry. Money, indeed, is not often in China withdrawn from circulation for the purpose of being hoarded; in fact, the habits of the Chinese are not parsimonious. Though the most actively industrious race of beings in the world, they are sensual and luxurious. Unlike the priest-ridden Hindoo, the son of Han pays but few taxes to the gods. Births, marriages and funerals, are in this country indeed, as elsewhere, made occasions of expense, but it is only at the death of a parent, when the property of the deceased furnishes the means, that institutions of a religious character are attended with any very considerable cost. Official rapacity renders the accumulation of wealth a dangerous experiment, while filial duty imposes on children the charge of maintaining their parents, and thus the Chinese are more distinguished by industry and enterprise in acquiring wealth, than by parsimony in the use of it. With this general inclination to spend, and the means of indulgence in the hands of so many members of the community, there is no want of commercial activity in bringing from abroad such objects of luxury as their own country cannot supply.

Mercantile speculation, indeed, accords well with the gambling disposition very generally prevalent among this people. The factors of the East India Company, writing to their employers in the year 1622, inform them in the quaint style of the day, that " Concerning the trade of China, three things are especially made known unto the world. The one is the abundance of trade it affordeth. The second is, that they admit no strangers into their country. The third is, that trade is as life unto the vulgar, which, in remote parts, they will seek and accommodate with hazard and all they have." The interesting and instructive narratives of Lindsay and Gutzlaff prove, that, after the lapse of two hundred years, those *three things* are, at the present hour, as strikingly characteristic of the nation as they ever were.

This commercial disposition is favoured by the possession of a range of sea-coast, which, stretching in a curvilinear course from the Island of Hainan on the south-west, to the Gulf of Leautong, through twenty-three degrees of latitude and thirteen degrees of longitude, presents to the mariner, in an extent of upwards of two thousand five hundred miles, numerous convenient harbours or safe roadsteads, whose shores abound with marts for every variety of merchandise, while the magnificent rivers and canals of the interior afford admirable facilities, not only for the interchange of domestic productions, but for the transport of foreign commodities to the most remote parts of the country.

Unlike the climate of Hindostan, that of China is subject to extreme vicissitudes of cold and heat. In the northern half of the empire indeed, the rigour of winter is as intense as in most parts of Europe, rendering similar precautions necessary to guard against its severity. But while warm clothing would be insupportable under the burning sun of the summer months, the Chinese does not, on that account, like the Hindoo, discard all covering from his body, but is content to wear fewer or lighter garments.

In a commercial point of view the political situation of China is more advantageous than that of Hindostan, inasmuch as the country is self-governed. Its produce is not sent abroad to defray the expense of a foreign government, but to be given in exchange for commodities which may administer to the wants or comforts of its own population, or to be returned with profits that increase the capital of its merchants.

With reference therefore to the importance of the trade with China to manufacturing interests, we cannot but feel regret as well as astonishment, that the apathy or indecision of our statesmen should have left our commercial relations with that nation in the deplorable state in which they are found at the present moment.

The British cotton manufacturer cannot forget that even the once far-famed fabrics of Bengal have given place to his superior skill, not only in the general market of the world, but in the very field of its production. Already have the nankins of China itself almost ceased to be numbered amongst its staple exports, unable to compete with the nankins of England. It seems, indeed, impossible that, drawing a part of his raw material from India at a very enhanced price, while the cost of his labour is more than double that of the Hindoo weavers, the Chinese could, any more than his Indian neighbours, clothe himself so cheaply or so well, in articles of his own manufacture as in those from the British loom, were the latter fairly placed within his reach. A population far exceeding that of all Europe is ready and able to purchase the productions of the British weavers. One Man* has been induced to say they shall not, and England has kissed the dust from his feet and acquiesced in humble silence.

Should a brighter day arrive, and the ports of China be freely opened to our woollens, it must be the fault of our manufacturers if they do not obtain possession of the most extensive market that has been ever presented to them; for China possesses neither the materials nor the skill that would enable it to compete with us. Unless, however, great exertions are made, continental Europe, by supplying

* The Emperor of China.

our many fabrics at a lower price, is not unlikely to occupy the better part of this vast field. Of glass ware in any shape there is no manufactory in China that deserves the name, so that in this branch also an almost boundless field is unoccupied. It is to be hoped that when the paralysing touch of the excise is withdrawn from our glass-works, we shall cease to be, as hitherto, undersold by competitors of other countries far less skilful than our own manufacturers.

The Chinese employed in our Indian foundries and dockyards have proved to be excellent workmen; but mere manual labour cannot compete with the powers of the steam-engine. The hardware of Sheffield and Birmingham must therefore one day supersede the native tools and cutlery of China. Surpassing, in short, the Chinese in every branch of art and science, as well as in capital and machinery, there is scarcely an article, food excepted, that can administer to the wants or tastes of man, that the manufacturers of England may not supply to them of a quality and at a price that will ensure an almost unlimited demand. It does not, indeed, seem too much to expect that even the porcelain of Keang Se may, at last, in China as in Europe, give place to the stone-ware of Worcestershire or Staffordshire; or that English silk stuffs may, at no distant period, be bartered for the raw silk of Kyang Nan.

Against the reality of such brilliant prospects, it may perhaps be urged, that experience shows them to be illusory. The East India Company say they made the most patriotic efforts to introduce British goods into China, but were unable, even at the willing sacrifice of large sums in the experiment, to force

any considerable quantity on that market. Nor is it
a sufficient answer to this fact, to allege, in explanation, the want of skill and economy that pervaded
every part of the trading system pursued by those
merchant-sovereigns. The enterprising traders of
the United States have also failed in this object,
though neither prudence nor judgment was wanting
in the attempt.

To this argument, there is an obvious and conclu-
sive reply. Neither the East India Company, nor
any other merchants, have as yet been permitted,
correctly speaking, to trade with China. Their
dealings have been conducted with about a dozen
individuals, whose residence, indeed, is in that
country, but who ought to be considered rather
in the light of slaves to the officers of the local
government, than as merchants. The experiment
cannot be regarded as fairly made, till the free-
trader can legitimately pursue the natural liberty
of trafficking where, with whom, and in what objects of commerce may best suit his interest; secure
from all molestation so long as he offends against no
rational law of the country, and sure of redress
should wrong be offered to him.

How different from such conditions are those
under which commerce with China has hitherto been
conducted! Obliged to limit their resort to a
single port, lying at a distance of fifteen hundred
miles from the capital, foreigners are even there
prohibited from dealing with any native who is not
of the privileged number of hong merchants, half
of whom are believed to be in insolvent circumstances.

It is found convenient by the officers of government to assume as a general axiom, that all foreigners are to be included among those who are described in their classical works as barbarians, incapable of appreciating the laws and institutions of a civilized people. They are, therefore, to be denied access to the regular tribunals of the country, and are placed under the guidance and control of those very men with whom alone they are allowed to have any dealings,—the merchant who buys from them, the comprador or steward who supplies their wants, and the linguist who interprets for them. As a counterpart arrangement flowing from the same principle, those hong merchants, linguists, and compradors are, in their turn, made responsible for the conduct of foreigners. The arbitrary system of authority under which they are from infancy brought up, makes those men far more submissive and tractable subjects to deal with than free-born Englishmen. Nor is there wanting a share of plausibility for this arrangement. Foreigners are ignorant of the laws of China, and may therefore chance to transgress them, though they can have no wish to infringe on the ordinances of the country which they make their temporary residence. It is the duty of those natives who are about them, and who are authorised to transact business with them, to direct them how to avoid such infringements. If foreigners err in this respect, it is from want of good advice, or from following bad advice ; and, therefore, it is but just that their officially appointed advisers shall be punished. But, from the use that is made of those provisions, it is easy to distinguish between their ostensible and their real pur-

pose; and what the latter is, will be but too well
developed as we proceed. In the mean time, we
may state that it is an avowed maxim of their commercial policy to prevent foreigners from acquiring a
knowledge of the real state of the market; as it is
the anxious care of the local authorities to stifle their
complaints : both which objects the arrangements
referred to are well calculated to secure. The limited number of those sponsors makes it at once easy
to select any individual among them, when a victim to rapacity is required; while the monopoly they
enjoy is supposed also to contract into a focus, as it
were, the means of gratifying that cupidity. Nor is
a plea for extortion ever wanting. Even to be liable
to the imputation of intimacy with foreigners is con-
structive treason ; so that, between the jealousy of
rivals and the extortions of his rulers, it is difficult
for a hong merchant, who aims at giving satisfaction to those with whom he has dealings, to escape
imprisonment and torture, except by the sacrifice of
all he may possess. It is not, therefore, surprising
that respectable persons can seldom be persuaded to
place themselves in a situation of such danger; but
it would be truly astonishing, if, under such circumstances, commerce could be conducted with vigour,
or be pushed to the extent of which it is capable.

But to see more clearly the position of the
Chinese, with respect to the foreign trade at
Canton, the British merchant has only to figure to
himself the consequences that would ensue to him,
were the Grand Seignior to become emperor of all
Europe, and to rigorously enjoin that its trade
with the rest of the world should be conducted at

the Porte, and no where else; that all transport of British goods by sea should be prohibited, lest foreigners might by that means receive their supplies without going to Constantinople, and that to carry on direct correspondence with an American or East Indian merchant should be deemed treasonable. Let him then imagine that, even after he has carried his goods up the Rhine, and down the Danube, and along the shores of the Euxine, till he has landed them at Constantinople, he is allowed to select, from among only a dozen privileged merchants, the one through whom he may choose to deal, and that he is entirely at the mercy of this man, both for the price which he may obtain for his goods, and the rate at which he must pay for his returns. This is precisely the position of the country merchant at Canton.

To the situation of the foreign merchant there, a parallel may be drawn, by supposing the American, in the preceding case, to be an object systematically held up to popular scorn, in public proclamations issued by the effendi; to be described in these as addicted to every vice, and to be of a class of beings with whom it is pollution to hold social intercourse; to be forbidden even to assume the appearance of fixing his residence in Turkey, by bringing to it his wife and family; to be debarred from quitting, for air or exercise, the barrack allotted to himself and his fellow-merchants, except at long intervals, and under the charge of a special guide, made responsible for his conduct; to be denied the privilege of using a conveyance in case of illness; to be precluded from hiring warehouses for his goods, and from treating with any unprivileged merchant for their sale; and yet to have no legitimate access to redress, should the person to whom they have been entrusted abscond without accounting for their value. Suffering under these indignities and restraints, our American merchant may derive what consolation he can, from knowing that the situation of those with whom he deals, is in some respects, more abject than his own; that they are never for an instant safe in their persons or property; that the only security they have against arbitrary banishment and confiscation is the caution of their rulers, not to cut off the source of their own habitual plunder; and that they have not the power of withdrawing themselves from their wretched position by renouncing trade.

That this is no overcharged picture of the conditions under which foreign trade is permitted at Canton, the reader may easily satisfy himself by reference to the documents relative to the subject, which have been, on different occasions, laid before committees of Parliament.

Various means have been resorted to, for the purpose of placing our commerce in China on a better footing; but bribery, embassies, and threats to abandon the trade altogether, have been tried with very partial or temporary advantage; and ministers have not hitherto considered the case as one for the remedy of which measures of coercion were expedient, or, perhaps, justifiable. Whether they have been right or wrong in this course of policy, it would be absurd to indulge in the expectation that, while the present system continues, the trade with China can be otherwise than an object of trivial importance to the merchants and manufacturers of Great Britain. Let every man, then, who regards the welfare of our country, intimately linked as is its prosperity with that of its commerce, bear in mind that, on the continuance or removal of these degrading and injurious restrictions, depends the almost entire exclusion of our manufactures from what is capable of becoming the first market for them in the world, or their admission into a new commercial field of such unbounded extent, that the mind can scarcely embrace the wide and magnificent view which it presents. Let all, then, who desire to promote the national industry in every branch, unite with one voice to rouse the ministry from the lethargy under which they appear to have slumbered, while the trade of China has claimed a share of their attention; and let them be urged to abandon the tame and truckling line of policy, which, from a groundless apprehension of danger to one branch of the revenue, has so long endured, to the disgrace of the British name, and to the sacrifice of our commercial interests.

Nor is there any time to be lost in awakening attention to this subject. The present occasion serves most opportunely for the adoption of measures that may at once retrieve the national honour, and pave the way for speedily placing our relations with China on a new and desirable footing. Our sovereign himself has, in the person of his representative at Canton, the late Lord Napier, been insulted by the Chinese authorities, and the national flag has been fired upon from Chinese batteries. It can

scarcely, perhaps, be apprehended that any of the
present ministers of the Crown will prove himself
so base, so lost to all sense of national honour, as to
recommend that England shall submit to such indignities; but it may be well that those who are so
deeply responsible to their country in such matters
should feel themselves supported by the loud ex-
pression of public opinion, in adopting such measures
as are calculated to ensure success.

The merchants at Canton have already, in the
form of a petition * to the Crown, pointed out the
objects which demand its notice, and the facility
with which they might be attained. It is not likely
that, among those who are competent to form a
correct opinion on this subject, there will be many
who will not concur in the views of the petitioners;
but, for the satisfaction of those less familiar with
Chinese insolence, rapacity, venality, mendacity,
and pusillanimity, it may be desirable to offer some
illustrations of the grounds on which those views
appear to have been adopted.

It has often been alleged, as an argument for the
duty of passive submission, on the part of foreigners,
to whatever treatment they may be subjected to by
the Chinese, that it has been, from time immemorial,
a standing rule of their policy to interdict the resort
of strangers to their ports, and that the exceptions
actually existing arise only from special indulgence,
subject, in each instance, to the condition that it
may be withdrawn at a moment, without any cause
being assigned. That this opinion, however true in
theory, is practically at variance not only with facts

* Given in the Appendix.

recorded by Chinese authors, but with the history of the British trade in particular, it will be easy to show. The Chinese have, in all ages, valued foreign trade; and our own has been established upon conditions voluntarily entered upon with the view of attracting it in the first instance, and not in the face of the repulsive obstacles that now obtain; though those terms have been violated or encroached upon by them from time to time, till it has frequently become a question whether it would not be better to incur at once the immense sacrifice of abandoning it altogether, rather than conduct it under the unfair and oppressive restrictions that have been subsequently imposed upon it.

By turning to the first volume of that valuable periodical, the Chinese Repository, published at Canton, we shall find mention made of several instances of foreign embassies to and *from* China, as well as of commercial intercourse with neighbouring nations from 2000 years B.C.; that from the time of Hwan Te, A.D. 176, trade with foreigners was carried on at Canton; but it was not until about A.D. 700, in the time of the Tang dynasty, that an Imperial commissioner was appointed to receive *fixed duties* there on behalf of Government. Extraordinary commodities and foreign manufactures were then imported to such an extent, as to induce the governors, in the year 705, to cut that famous pass through the Mei Lin chain, which forms, to this day, the route of all commerce between Canton and the more northern parts of the empire.

Rapacity, however, soon began to be displayed by the local government. In 795, the chief officer in command at Canton, stated to the Court that the foreign merchants had deserted the port, and had repaired to the neighbouring coast of Cochin China. He thereupon proposed to the emperor to send a sort of consul thither to bring them back. Some of the ministers were in favour of the measure, but the Imperial will was determined in opposition to it by the opinion of one who argued to this effect:— " Multitudes of trading vessels have heretofore flocked to Canton. If they have, all at once, deserted it, and repaired to Cochin China, it must have been either from extortions being insupportable, or from some failure in affording proper inducements. When a gem spoils in the case, who is to be blamed but the keeper of it ? If the pearl be fled to other regions, how is it to be propelled back again? The Shoo King says, ' Do not prize too much (do not assess too highly) strange commodities, and persons will soon come from remote parts.'"

In the thirteenth century it appears that the rate of duty was ten per cent. on the value of goods.

In 1300, the first emperor of the Yuen dynasty sent an embassy to the king of Japan. In his letter he said, " The sages consider the whole world as one family ; but if all the members have not a friendly intercourse, how can it be said that the principle of one family is maintained ? " Nothing can be more just than this principle ; and all that can be desired with respect to China, is to see it practically applied in her intercourse with other states.

This embassy was not allowed to land ; but afterwards Hung Woo, an emperor of the Ming dynasty, sent a priest of Buddha who had better success.

One of the points on which he was directed by his instructions to insist, was " the ancient law of universal and equal benevolence to all, whether remote or near at hand."

These quotations show that *isolation* from all the world, the anti-social system as regards other nations, so far from being a fundamental principle of Chinese political ethics, as has been constantly repeated, till it has come to be received as an unquestionable truth, is, on the contrary, at direct variance with the authorities on which their political creed is avowedly founded.

The contrary doctrine, which would exclude the Chinese from the society of nations, would divest them of all claim to the protection of international law. Variously distributed as are the gifts of nature over the several regions of the earth, it is only by the interchange of commodities that the inhabitants of each portion can severally have their due share of the bounty prepared for all who, by their industry, are entitled to participate in the common stock. If then there should be any government which should, as China has been supposed to do, capriciously set itself against the general good, in opposition to the desires of its own subjects as well as the demands of its neighbours, it can have but little claim to their consideration and forbearance. It must be regarded, *quoad hoc*, as the common wrong of mankind, and as such be compelled to abandon a position so hostile to the general interests of the human race. The practical recognition of the contrary principle, as we have seen, is a fact which cannot for a moment be forgotten, should the stipulations we may propose be objected to, on the pretext of ancient custom being opposed to their admission.

In the fourteenth century the provinces of Che Këang, Fuh Këen, and Kwang Tung were appointed for the reception of foreign ships. Merchants wishing to go to other ports were allowed to do so, on giving a bond to carry no prohibited articles. This also is a precedent which must not be lost sight of where antiquity stands for reason.

The Portuguese first visited China in 1517. They were received with friendship and readily admitted to trade. They formed several establishments along the coast, but their conduct was far from being marked with moderation. They erected forts, and particularly at Formosa, laid taxes and contributions upon the inhabitants, and levied duties upon all junks that came in their way, as if they had been sovereigns of the country. To show how little the exclusion of strangers was practically the law of the land at that time, it may be mentioned that as early as 1533 they carried on from Ningpo, in Che Këang, a most flourishing trade with Japan; so that when, twelve years afterwards, the place was taken by storm by the provincial government, in consequence of some rebellious conduct of the inhabitants, there were said to be among the slain twelve thousand Christians, of whom eight thousand were Portuguese, and thirty-five of their ships were burnt in the harbours. They afterwards formed a settlement at Chinchew, on the coast of Fokien, from which, in 1549, they were expelled for their violence and misconduct; as they were a second time from Ningpo, but at what date is uncertain. It would appear that

c

it was about the year 1557 they were permitted to
establish themselves at Macao, on condition of paying tribute and custom for their merchandise. Five
years before, when the celebrated missionary Xavier
arrived at the Island of San Shan, or St. John's,
near the entrance to the river of Canton, he found
them still at that, their original station. Their previous misconduct had already led to the exclusion of
foreigners from the interior; and the apostle, as he is
called, could, for some time, get no one to undertake
to convey him to Canton, till, at last, a Chinese
merchant was induced to engage to land him there
by night. He did not live however to make the
experiment.

The conduct of the Dutch, who followed the Portuguese, though a century later, and who too closely
imitated their example, was not calculated to restore
foreigners to the favourable opinion of the Chinese.
They are accused of various acts of violence and
piracy,—the latter under the English flag. They
took forcible possession of one of the Pescadore
Islands, but, on condition of its relinquishment, were
permitted to form a settlement at Tywan on Formosa,
and allowed the privilege of general trade with
China. Thirty-eight years afterwards they were
driven from Formosa by a Chinese rebel to the Tartar
dynasty, which ascended the throne in 1664.

The Spaniards were content to trade at Emoy and
Macao, as they have still permission to do; but
the English found themselves, for a long time, excluded from all the ports of China, in consequence, as
they allege, of the intrigues of the Portuguese and
Dutch, their precursors and rivals. At length, in the

year 1635, the Presidency at Surat received a proposition from the Portuguese viceroy at Goa, for a truce and a free trade to Macao and all other Portuguese settlements. A treaty was accordingly drawn up, which was confirmed by the kings of Spain and England. In consequence of this compact Captain Weddell was sent out on the part of a new trading association, in which Charles the First himself had shares, with four ships, and carrying a letter from the king to the captain-general of Macao, with a view of opening a trade with China at that place, and if possible at Canton. The Portuguese gave the English a very unsatisfactory reception, alleging their own apprehension of giving offence to the Chinese. This induced Captain Weddell to try the effect of negotiation at Canton. With this view he despatched two of the supercargoes of the ships in a barge, accompanied by an armed pinnace, to explore the river and find a passage to the city. Pursuing this intent, they fell in with a fleet of twenty sail of Chinese war junks, the admiral of which at first interrogated them very roughly as to who they were, whence they came, whither they were going, and with what object. Having given him satisfactory answers on these points, he became gradually more civil, but begged of them not to take the pinnace on any farther, offering to lend them a junk of his own fleet for their conveyance to Canton. This offer the supercargoes accepted. The news, however, of their progress had preceded them, and some leagues below Canton they were met by messengers, who said they came from the hoppo, and other mandarins, with a request that they would return to Macao, promising, on their compliance, that those officers would assist them in procuring from the viceroy liberty to trade. They returned to Macao accordingly; but after waiting ten or twelves days without farther communication from Canton, Captain Weddell resolved on moving his ships up the river. He advanced till he came near a dismantled fort or castle, as it was called, where some men-of-war junks lay. Some mandarins on board of them promised to procure him permission to trade if he would remain there for six days till an answer to their application could arrive from Canton. The interval was employed by the Chinese to mount guns on the batteries of the fort, and, on the fourth day, a boat going from the ships for water was fired upon. Incensed at this unprovoked outrage, Captain Weddell's fleet weighed anchor and ascended with the flood to take a position in front of the fort, where several shots were discharged at the ships before they could get their guns to bear. The action lasted two hours, when the courage of the Chinese being observed to fail, a hundred men were landed in the ships' boats.

The Chinese immediately fled in great confusion; forty-six iron guns were taken possession of, and carried on board the ships; the council-house, as it is called, was fired, and other buildings demolished. After seizing some junks, which were afterwards released on his receiving overtures of peace from the Chinese, Captain Weddell was at last permitted to send the supercargoes to Canton, that they might petition for trade. They were there received with great honour by the chumpeen, who severely blamed the Portuguese for what had occurred, and professed himself the sincere friend of Captain Weddell's people! After three days the supercargoes were enabled to return to their ships with a *patent for free trade, and liberty to fortify on any place outside of the mouth of the river.*

The guns taken from the fort were now restored, and trading commenced; but while all was going on prosperously and peaceably, one of the supercargoes was suddenly arrested on his way to Canton with money and goods, and was confined on board a junk. Seven fire junks were at the same time sent down by night to destroy the English fleet, but they were fortunately avoided and burnt. Two supercargoes who were residing at Canton were confined in their house; their domestics were expelled,—their fire was quenched, victuals were denied them, and a guard of soldiers was placed over them to prevent all access. Having sustained themselves for two or three days on a little biscuit and arrack, they became at last desperate. They heaped up some billets of wood into piles, and ignited one of them by means of a burning lens; and being thereon questioned as to their intentions, they replied, that having been treacherously used, they meant to avenge themselves by setting fire to the town.

This threat procured them the liberty of open doors, but the guard of soldiers was still kept over them. Notwithstanding this, one of them, with a sword in one hand and money in the other, made several sallies on passengers carrying provisions, which he seized, but paid for, and thus saved himself and fellow-prisoners from starvation.

Captain Weddell and his followers, in the mean

time, hearing that the supercargoes were imprisoned, resolved to release them, or lose their lives in the attempt; and, accordingly, with his ships' boats, he set upon sixteen men-of-war junks, burnt five, and dispersed the rest. They next fell upon the neighbouring towns and villages, burning and destroying wherever they went. The inhabitants fled to Canton to complain, and this produced the desired effect. The supercargoes were released; apologies and complimentary messages were sent to them by the principal authorities, and the blame of the treatment they had received was cast upon their broker, who was imprisoned and bambooed. The perfidious conduct of the Chinese is attributed to the intrigues of the Portuguese at Macao, who are alleged to have expended 80,000 taels, (23,000*l*.) in bribes to the hoppo and other officers, that they might prevent the English from participating in the trade. Of their hostile feeling towards Captain Weddell's expedition, their whole conduct afforded proofs sufficient to sustain the probability of their having so acted.

It is stated, that, after their release, the supercargoes and their people enjoyed great liberty at Canton, till their final despatch; and that they were promised ample trade and residence for the future, on condition of a yearly payment of 2000 taels, four pieces of iron ordnance, and fifty muskets. Captain Weddell selected a situation for a fort; but the association to which he belonged became so embarrassed by the hostilities of the Dutch, and still more by those of their own countrymen of the East India Company, that they were unable to prosecute Captain Weddell's plans.

The generous and manly conduct of the Portuguese at Macao to our countrymen, on a late occasion,* affords a pleasing contrast to the behaviour of their predecessors in the time of Captain Weddell; but the Chinese of the nineteenth century have proved themselves the same false, venal, cowardly, and treacherous race as those of the seventeenth.

That the blood of English seamen has not degenerated, we have ample proofs; and it is not their fault that the example of Captain Weddell and his resolute associates was forgotten, as it appears to have been, when the king's commissioner was left to pine in sickness at Canton, a prisoner in his house, while his domestics were expelled, his fire was quenched, victuals denied him; and a guard of Chinese soldiers were put over the factory to prevent all communication between him and the king's ships in the river.

When, indeed, his majesty's ships were fired upon from the castles, they bravely returned the fire and passed up; but no force was landed to take the forts and carry off the guns; no junks were captured, nor hostages taken for the safety of his majesty's representative at Canton. Fifty merchant ships bearing the British flag, several of them well armed, lay at anchor above or below the forts, but not a boat's crew nor a man from them was moved in the national cause. Who can doubt, that had a different course been pursued — had the spirited and honourable resolution that led the men of 1637 to

---

* During the late Lord Napier's discussions with the Canton government.

rescue their countrymen at the peril of their lives, been adopted by the commanders of the king's and merchant ships of 1834, their success would have been similar, though far more important in its result? Some unfortunate linguist or wealthy hong merchant might, as then, have been made a scapegoat by the Chinese authorities; but numerous apologies and complimentary messages would have been sent from the viceroy to Lord Napier, whom he would have been proud to acknowledge as the honoured guest of his country. The fact of not receiving his letter would have been anxiously explained as a mistake, to be atoned for by ample liberty to correspond with his Excellency for the future. The national honour would have remained unstained by the disgraceful spectacle of its representative being treacherously, and contrary to compact, sent *as a prisoner* from Canton to Macao, by a circuitous passage, *wilfully* and *needlessly prolonged for several days;* that, labouring as his lordship was under a fever, he might be subjected to the most injurious annoyances. Lord Napier's valuable life might have been saved, and the intrigues of the hong merchants, like those of the Portuguese of former days, defeated. Both were aimed at the prevention of a new order of things, that threatened danger to their respective monopolies. Those intrigues once foiled, his lordship's zeal and address might, without farther military effort, have succeeded in placing our commerce with China on a more desirable footing even than was conceded to Captain Weddell. He might have obtained *free* and *ample residence* for British merchants in every part of China, instead of the single port of Canton,

and other immunities far more valuable than the
liberty of *fortifying* on any island wheresoever.

These reflections are not offered with the view of
casting blame on the naval officer who commanded
on the occasion. He no doubt went to the full extent of the request preferred to him by Lord
Napier, from whom he could not receive any fresh
communication after his lordship had begun to be
subjected to the indignities already described; and
prior to these nothing had occurred to call for such
vigorous measures as afterwards became desirable.
It is only to be regretted that, under the altered circumstances, and the unexpected delay in getting
the frigates up to Whampoa, he should still, for
want of such communication, have considered himself not warranted to depart from the line of conduct first contemplated, and have hesitated to take
steps for the immediate opening up of a direct and
certain communication with his lordship by means
of the ships' boats, especially as he had the second
Commissioner on board, on his way to rejoin Lord
Napier.

But the gallantry of both Captains Blackwood
and Chads is too well established to admit of a
doubt that their quiescence was most painful to themselves, and only submitted to as obligatory under
the heavy responsibility that would have attached
to more active measures, while there existed the
remotest chance of those proving unsuccessful.

Returning from this digression, it may be well to
pursue the history of the British trade with China a
little farther, that we may trace the origin and growth
of the restrictions and impositions under which that
commerce now labours; and then be better able to

judge of the practicability of obtaining for it a more advantageous position, without subjecting ourselves to the reproach of effecting that object by doing violence to the fundamental principles on which that singular country is governed.

At the period of Captain Weddell's expedition, the Imperial authority had scarcely more weight in the provinces of China than was, during those same times, attached to the royal prerogative in England.

The principle of admission to trade was, therefore, accorded or withheld as suited the views or the interests of the provincial authorities, who also usurped the right of adjusting the duties in each particular case. There is reason, however, to believe that the established customs on foreign trade had for ages been of two kinds,—a measurement charge on vessels according to their dimensions, and a fixed duty on each sort of goods, according to the respective descriptions which were then usually brought to market.

It does not appear that Captain Weddell's four ships were subjected to any measurement or other specific duty. They paid 10,000 Spanish dollars as a gross sum, in lieu of all charges, being 2500 Spanish dollars for each ship. In this case it is probable that the purchaser paid the established duties on goods. It would seem, however, that the London, which had traded to Macao two years before under a charter from Goa, had paid 1400 dollars measurement duty. For some time subsequently, the trade to this part of China seems to have been carried on principally by private ships, of whose proceedings we have no records. But in 1644, the Honourable

Company's ship Hinde was obliged to pay 3500 dollars measurage, though, in proportion to the London, she ought to have paid only 800 dollars. Twenty years afterwards, the Surat frigate was rated at 2000 taels (2750 dollars), which the supercargo refusing to pay, she left the port. In 1680, there appears to have been an invitation from the governor of Canton to establish a factory there; to which, however, it was not deemed prudent to accede. The Company had previously carried on trade at Emoy and Formosa, on the invitation of Coxinga, a Chinese pirate then exercising sovereignty in defiance of the Imperial Tartar Government.

In 1682, the Portuguese are alleged to have paid the viceroy of Canton 24,000 taels (33,333 dollars,) for the privilege of exclusive foreign trade. This, which was to have been an annual payment, was probably not often repeated. In 1689, the ship Defence escaped an overcharge in measurement by a bribe to the measurers: 2484 taels (3450 dollars) were demanded, which was compromised for a payment of 1500 taels, of which 300 went as a bribe to the hoppo and his officers. At this time occurred the first instance of a homicide. A Chinese having been shot in a fray, in which some unarmed Englishmen fell into their hands, and were cruelly put to death, 5000 taels were demanded as an atonement: 2000 were actually offered, but not accepted. The ship sailed without coming to an adjustment.

In 1684, the Delight went to Emoy, after the province had been finally reduced by the Tartars; and Formosa also had been surrendered to them by

the grandson of the famous Coxinga, who had in
1662 expelled the Dutch from that island. This
voyage of the Delight was undertaken at the express
invitation of a mandarin of high rank, styled Ta Laou
Yay, Chung Kung. No steps, however, were allowed to be taken towards trading until presents were
made to the mandarins: some of whom unblushingly
rejected them as too small, and required larger. The
supercargoes were then told that the viceroy was disposed to allow them to trade, but that their brass guns,
muskets, and powder must be presented to the emperor. It was also agreed that for 1100 taels worth
of goods they should be allowed to take possession
of the factory that had been occupied by the English while Emoy was in the hands of the rebels.
The same amount was then demanded in cash, together with twelve pieces of fine broad-cloth. Although this was duly paid, they were ordered to
re-embark forthwith, that the factory might be
given to the Dutch, who were then in favour. The
English were obliged to give place accordingly,
having expended 2000*l.* to no purpose, except obtaining a promise that they would be allowed free
trade if they returned the following year. The brass
guns, &c. were forcibly taken from the factory,
though none of the conditions on which they were
to have been given had been fulfilled. Proceeding
on the promise made to the Delight, the ships China,
Merchant and Adventurer went to Emoy the following year, and obtained what was called a king's
chop for free trade; but refusing to make large presents, their trade was interdicted. The general
named See, Ta Laou Yay, who had returned after

negotiating with the king of Formosa for his submission to the emperor, recommended an embassy to Pekin. He assured them, at the same time, that he had obtained for them the viceroy's permission to trade. This, which demanded a present in acknowledgment, proved to be a falsehood. Large sums were at last expended in presents, and the death of a Chinese by the hands of one of the men of the Adventurer, was compromised by farther presents to the general and other mandarins.

The measurement charge at Emoy, as at Canton, appears to have been at this time quite arbitrary. The New London was rated at 1,147 taels, while the Worcester had paid only 612.

In 1689, it is recorded that the mandarins at Emoy, after making enormous exactions on the supercargoes of the ship Princess, put them in confinement, from which they were not released till they made farther heavy payments as bribes or presents. The supercargo of the Cooke was chained in his factory, and obliged to take whatever goods were offered, leaving 20,400 taels unrecovered. One might have thought that treatment such as this would have produced demonstrations of resentment in some form stronger than words. The Court's instructions of this period, however, earnestly enjoined forbearance from all conduct that might be displeasing to the Chinese! Those acts of extortion and violence were, in consequence, submitted to without any attempt at resistance or retaliation. That it should have been enjoined on all persons in their employ, to abstain from giving just cause of offence to the Chinese, or other nation, would have been but proper. But had they, at the same time, been directed not to submit quietly to insult or injury for the sake of commercial advantage, they might have been more successful in escaping those extortions and oppressions, which at last forced them to abandon Emoy, as well as other ports; and might have been enabled to conduct their trade with China generally, more profitably and securely than they were ever able to do under a submissive and so called conciliatory system.

In 1702, the hoppo of Canton bambooed a linguist, because the supercargoes of some ships refused to let a proclamation be pasted on their door till they knew what were its contents. It proved to be a prohibition from dealing with them without a license from the hoppo, which was to be granted only to those who agreed to pay him five per cent. on their contracts. On payment of 3900 taels, this restriction was withdrawn. This is the earliest case recorded of the practical application of the plan for punishing barbarians by proxy.

The foreign trade was, about this time, both at Emoy and Canton, granted by the government as a monopoly to a single privileged merchant. Having, however, neither goods nor money at his command, he relinquished his monopoly for a payment of 5000 taels (1650*l.*) per ship. In 1704 a new duty was exacted of four per cent., of which we have the following account. One per cent. had, for the two previous seasons, been allowed by the merchants to the linguists in their contracts, out of which the linguist paid the hoppo for his appointment. The other three per cent. had been exacted from the merchants by the

hoppo, for permission to trade ; the merchants escaping half the charge, however, by undervaluing the
goods generally, and altogether concealing some part.

Exactions were now carried to such a height, that
the Company ceased for two years from sending any
ships to Canton, as they had previously, for similar
reasons, withdrawn from Emoy. An attempt, in
1701, to open a trade at Chusan, an island on the coast
of the province of Che Këang, was frustrated from the
same cause. The sum of 10,000*l.* appears to have been
expended in bribes and presents ; and 51,000 taels
(17,000*l.*) of debt due by Chinese merchants remained unrecovered the first year. The following
year 10,000 taels were paid to the hoppo for permission to trade, and afterwards 6000 taels addi-
tional for confirming that permission. In 1710-11
the Rochester, touching at Emoy, on her voyage to
Chusan, was strongly pressed to remain ; the mandarins promising to subscribe to whatever terms
might be required. This offer, however, was not
availed of, and the Rochester proceeded on her
voyage. At Chusan the mandarins at first held out
every encouragement and facility ; but, in the end,
the supercargoes were compelled by main force to
receive goods for which they had not contracted ;
and exactions were made by the mandarins on all
purchases, down to vegetables for the factory table.
Chusan was abandoned, and not revisited for many
years.

In 1712, the Company's ships coming to Canton
took the precaution of remaining near Macao till they
had settled a specific sum for measurage, presents,
and fees. They also stipulated for liberty to trade

with whom they pleased, and to choose their own
linguists and servants. They were promised exemption from all new customs and impositions; and had
granted to them the sole right of punishing their own
people if disorderly. It was also agreed that their
boats should not be stopped at the custom-houses,
and that they should be protected from all insults
and impositions on the part of the natives.

Such were the conditions on which we agreed to
give the Chinese the benefit of our commerce, when
it first assumed a regular form; and those stipulations were for some years required and acceded to on
the arrival of each fleet. It is, therefore, a misap-
prehension of the real case, and one which may to
some seem an error of great importance, to assume
that the trade was sought only on one side. The
facts we have stated show that the desire was mutual, and the conditions reciprocal; and the whole
subsequent history of our connexion with China is
compatible only with this view of the case. It is
true that those covenants were, in the first instance,
entered into with only subordinate officers without
legal authority; but we shall soon see that they
subsequently received the imperial sanction; and the
only defect in this treaty of commerce arose from
the inequality of the parties,—a despotic monarch
being the contractor on one side, and the servants of
a company of merchants, instead of their king, the
parties on the other.

In spite, however, of the stipulations acceded to
by the mandarins, and of the understanding that no
duties were at that time payable by the native merchants, those who dealt with foreigners were still

subjected to irregular exactions, or downright extortions that recoiled on the trade. To these generally no resistance was made; but, in the year 1716, a private ship, the Ann, of Madras, took possession of a junk belonging to Emoy, in satisfaction of some injuries received at that port. The emperor, being informed of this act of violence, sent a special commissioner to inquire into the affair; and, on his report, ordered the mandarins, whose duty it was to have seen justice done to the Madras merchants, to be severely punished. The value of the junk was eighty thousand taels; the whole demands of the Ann did not exceed fifteen thousand taels. The mandarins were obliged to make satisfaction to the owners of the junk, and the remainder of their property was confiscated. The good effects of the seizure by the Ann upon the conduct of the local functionaries were noticed for two succeeding seasons; yet the Company's supercargoes, acting upon the submissive and conciliating plan laid down for their guidance, do not appear to have profited by this example. There were some encroachments, however, of a tendency so vitally injurious to the trade as to rouse them to a passive resistance. The year 1720 is memorable as having given birth to the first association in the shape of a cohong, or exclusive company for foreign trade. This was formed under the auspices of the hoppo. He prohibited all but a few principal merchants from trading with the English; obliging all merchants not belonging to the society to pay a duty of twenty per cent. on China-ware, and forty per cent. on teas sold by them. The Te Tuh, or commander-in-chief, was said to be connected with this society. Under these

D

circumstances, the supercargoes resolutely withheld the ships from entering the port till this association should be dissolved, and, at the same time, applied to the viceroy for his interference. Their appeal received immediate attention, for the importance of the trade was well known and felt. Summoning the members of the cohong before him, he threatened that, if they did not dissolve the association, he would find means to compel them. The conspiracy was thus defeated for the time, and the trade was renewed. Another instance of successful reliance on the value set upon the Company's trade occurred soon afterwards. A person in the employment of the hoppo was accidentally killed at Whampoa, by some of the crew of the Bonito, a private ship from Madras. The trade of the Company was suspended ; the second mate and four inferior officers of the Cadogan, a Company's ship, were seized at Canton, and, after being led through the streets, were beaten by order of a mandarin under the Te Tuh. The factory was at the same time surrounded by soldiers, without any reason being assigned. The supercargoes, on this, intimated to the hoppo their resolution, that unless apology was made for this violence, they would recommend it to the Company to withdraw their commerce altogether from the port. They also made to the viceroy a representation of this insult and violation of their privileges, and demanded redress. The mandarin, who was the immediate instrument of those tyrannical proceedings, was in consequence degraded, deprived of his office, and bambooed. He was a colonel or commander of one thousand men.

It does not appear that any farther notice was

taken of the homicide in which this dispute originated. Another case is recorded, which was adjusted by the payment of a sum of money. The gunner's mate of another Madras ship accidentally shot a boy in a rice-field. The parties belonging to the vessel compromised the matter by a payment of two thousand taels, of which sum only three hundred and fifty taels went to the parents of the child. The governor, however, who really seems to have exhibited a rare instance of official probity for a Chinese functionary, was, it is said, for some time troublesome, alleging that the city magistrate and the Foo Yuen, or lieutenant-governor, had concerted a false story to the prejudice of the honour of the emperor; the usual practice when those officers have been bribed for forbearance. This is the fourth case on record of homicide, without life for life being demanded.

A Chinese scholar, who writes in the Repository as one master of his subject, says, "There are some cases which occurred many years ago, quoted in the Leu Le, whereon the emperor Keën Lung declared that, *in order to intimidate foreigners*, the local government of Canton should require *life for life*, without regard to the extenuating circumstances which the Chinese laws admitted when natives only were concerned." This provision, which may find its parallel perhaps in the slave-code of Jamaica, affords a fine illustration of what there may be in a name. Foreigners are *Man Ee*, that is, *fierce barbarians*. It is therefore necessary to bridle their ferocity by laws more sanguinary than are required for people within the pale of civilization. Criminal intention is held to be a necessary ingredient with other circumstances to constitute guilt in the case of a native; but that shall always be assumed in the case of a foreigner, whatever proof there may exist that the misfortune was purely accidental. Four instances of judicial murder under this law have proved it to be no dead letter; and among those the blood of two innocent Englishmen still cries out on their countrymen for their supine submission to an appellation, which has afforded pretext for the adoption of a spirit of legislation towards them that has led to such fatal results.

The viceroy of 1720 having been recalled, was succeeded by one who seems to have entered readily into all the avaricious schemes of the other mandarins. In 1723 the supercargoes of the Walpole, learning on their arrival at Macao, that the viceroy and most of the other great officers at Canton engrossed the whole trade, obliging the merchants to take large sums of money from them at exorbitant interest, or to give up the best part of their profits, and that they purchased tea in the country, and forced the merchants to take it at their own price, refused to trade while commerce remained on that footing. Almost all the native merchants engaged in the foreign trade had been by this time ruined; and not more than two or three were in a condition to undertake a contract. The ship remained below till the supercargoes adjusted terms with the hoppo. It is stated that he granted all that was demanded, except that a duty of six per cent. should be taken off. This is the first time that this duty has been noticed in the published records, so that we have no clue to its nature or origin. It appears that the extortions practised by officers of the customs, had now become so notorious as to have reached the ears of the emperor Yung Ching, who in 1725 published the first tariff of duties, in the shape of a code, the strict observance of which was enjoined on the officers of all the custom-houses. They, however, in utter disregard of the express provisions of the code, took successful precautions for withholding from foreigners the useful information which this prohibition was calculated to convey to them. So heavy indeed had the exactions of the mandarins now become, that many of the native merchants forsook Canton, and went to Emoy, whither they invited the English to follow them; alleging, as an inducement, that the mandarins of that port were anxious for their return. The Company accordingly in 1727 sent instructions for the re-establishment of a factory at Emoy, addressing a letter to one of the principal merchants at Canton explaining their intentions. This invitation alarming the lieutenant-governor and hoppo, the former pledged himself to show the English the greatest favour if they would continue to trade at Canton; and the hoppo subscribed to the points urged by the supercargoes, that neither they nor the merchants whom they dealt with should pay higher or other duties, either for ships' measurage or goods, than the rates fixed by the emperor. The removal to Emoy was accordingly postponed. The respite thus obtained, however, was short. The very next year a new duty of ten per cent. was laid on all goods sold by the merchants, and none were allowed to be shipped except in the names of certain individuals. The supercargoes of the Company's ships, attended by the Madras, Bombay, and French mercantile gentlemen at Canton, found their way to the viceroy, to whom they delivered an address on the subject of their complaints. Their only satisfaction was being told, that it was proper they should deal with none but respectable merchants, and that they must pay the customs. A second time in 1728 the supercargoes broke through the guard to obtain an interview with the viceroy. They found only the chungya, as he is styled, a considerable mandarin, in attendance. Their linguist had refused to accompany them. The chungya found fault with them for not having brought him, and desired them to send for him, when they stated his refusal to obey them. On this the chungya gave orders that the linguist should be called; when it was discovered that both he and the merchants of whose conduct they had come to complain were all the while within. The supercargoes were told that they ought to apply to the hong merchants to obtain a hearing for them when necessary, but that they must not trouble the officers of government with every trifling matter. It was in vain that the supercargoes urged that the merchants would not obtain for them an opportunity of preferring a complaint against themselves. They could not be allowed to have unrestricted admission to the city, and thereby obtain, what they called, free access to justice. The emperor had ordered that no strangers should have that liberty. Whether this latter assertion was true or not, the right of access to justice has, though occasionally conceded when firmly insisted upon, been generally refused; and sometimes the resort to it has been prohibited under severe denunciations. Even under the most corrupt administration, oppression does not like to be shown its own deformity.

In 1734, the supercargoes, threatening to go to Emoy, were once more induced to remain by fair promises : one of which was, that the present, or *cumsha* of 1950 taels per ship, which had for some years been regularly exacted, should not in future be demanded.

At Emoy itself a renewal of trade from England direct was attempted. The supercargoes, upon anchoring in the outer harbours, received a favourable message and fair promises from the lieutenant-governor. At a conference with persons on the part of the hoppo, the privileges required were acceded to ; but it was with great difficulty that information could be obtained of the amount of the imperial duties, on which the hoppo's demand was limited to twenty per cent. Equal reluctance was shown to the production of the cubit by which the ships were to be measured. When brought, it was found only 11¼ inches in length, instead of 14⅝ : 1250 taels were required as measurement charge instead of 504, the legal amount; which, however, was ultimately accepted, but with the addition of twenty per cent. to the hoppo. The mandarins, however, reverted to their former practices. The hoppo, contrary to express stipulation, insisted on placing a person within the factory, to take account of all goods, to whom sold, &c. It was also demanded, that the guns, sails, powder, &c. should be brought on shore, and delivered up. The native merchants professed themselves to be deterred from trading, by apprehensions of the extortions of the hoppo and other mandarins. At length, it was resolved to inform the Te Tuh that unless a different course was enforced upon the inferior officers, the ships must leave the place. To Yan, as he is called, a great mandarin, promised to rectify some of the misconduct complained of. At length, a grand chop from the viceroy of the province arrived, directing that the English should be allowed full liberty to trade; stating that, by a decree of the imperial grand council, published four years before, the mandarins of Emoy are expressly enjoined not to demand a duty of seven per cent. formerly paid there by all European ships; it being hoped that, by this concession, they might again be induced to resort to Emoy to trade. Notwithstanding this, the imperial wishes were completely frustrated by the infamous conduct of the hoppo and other officers, "full of delays and prevarications, denying one day what they had been promised the day before." The result of all was, that the ships departed with the cargoes they had brought.

No sooner was this known at Canton, than the cumsha of 1950 taels, which it was promised to relinquish, was again insisted upon. Silks inferior to muster were fearlessly presented for delivery, and all former abuses repeated. It is now known, from the official custom-house book already alluded to, that, till between the year 1726 and 1729, the charges for cumsha, per centages of various descriptions, peculage, or allowances for weighing, and allowances for bringing silver to standard, &c. &c. had been levied by the custom-house officers for their private emolument. In the first year of Keën Lung,

(1736,) those charges underwent a revision, and were again amended in 1748; at which time it was specially enjoined on the viceroy of Canton that he should "print copies of the tariff of fees thus corrected, and have them openly announced and published; that lawless officers might not extort money beyond what was appointed, thereby annoying the mercantile people." This injunction was and has been totally disregarded.

Another attempt to trade at Emoy was made in 1735. It also failed, owing to exorbitant exactions and general injurious treatment; the mandarins by their conduct justifying the description given of them, that they could only be characterized as "devils in human shape." The supercargoes stated that the trade had no advantages that could compensate for the rapacity of the avaricious governors, and it was abandoned accordingly.

The last vessel that resorted to Emoy, went there to avoid the Spaniards who were cruising off Macao. After much time spent in fruitless discussions, she was obliged to quit the port, and proceeded to Bengal for a cargo. These facts are stated to remove a mistaken impression which has obtained currency, —that the English were expelled from Emoy for misconduct; than which idea nothing can be more wide of the truth.

Disappointed at Emoy, the attention of the Company was again directed to Chusan, or the neighbouring port of Ningpo; and, after an interval of twenty-five years from the last attempt, a vessel was sent there in 1736. Heavy duties, arbitrary and haughty conduct towards the supercargoes, extortions, and ruinous delays, are stated as the causes of failure, which seems to have been complete.

Had a proper representation of those abuses been conveyed to the emperor, there can be little doubt that redress would have been obtained. The edict published at Emoy proved that the cabinet of that time was well disposed towards the promotion of foreign trade, and to the removal of any obstacles to its prosecution that were brought under their cognizance. The difficulty was to find means of communicating with the court on the subject of wrongs committed by the very parties who were the regular channels for the transmission of petitions. The mandarins might perhaps have been driven by the complaints of Chinese subjects to bring the conduct of foreigners before government, had violent resistance been offered under which individuals had suffered injury; but no one had courage to repeat the experiment made by the Ann, and those wrongs remained unknown to the government, and therefore passed unpunished. It would appear, however, that the supercargoes at Canton had succeeded in drawing the attention of the emperor to the recent ten per cent. duty, for it was revoked in 1736 by an edict of Keën Lung, on the occasion of his accession, or rather his coronation at the conclusion of his minority. As the English were joined by the French in the remonstrance that had been offered, it is not improbable that they were partly indebted for this indulgence to the intercession of the jesuits, who were in great favour with the prince. The governor of Canton however took to himself the credit of the revocation, for which he demanded an *honorarium* of

30,000 taels,—"For why," said he, "should courtiers serve the English for nothing?" An advance of 6000 taels was made on bond to a merchant, on condition of his obtaining, in like manner, the revocation of an imperial order, that all ships should land their arms and ammunition. That order does not appear to have been repealed, but it was never afterwards acted on. It was discovered that the duty of ten per cent. had been represented to the emperor in the first instance as a voluntary contribution from the European merchants. Upon attending, according to invitation, to hear the edict read, the supercargoes were required to kneel, but they unanimously resisted. No audience of the viceroy could, however, afterwards be obtained without the ceremony of kneeling. The English in one address, presented through the viceroy, thanked the emperor for his favours; and in another solicited the removal of other burdens on their trade, but unsuccessfully. The measurement duty and cumsha were ordered still to be paid.

In 1741 a new Foo Yuen, or deputy-governor, attempted the renewal of former grievances; but, all the European merchants agreeing to suspend the trade till these were removed, the obnoxious orders were withdrawn.

This year was rendered remarkable by the arrival of Lord Anson, whose ship required to be provisioned and refitted. Supplies being at first withheld, the commodore determined to proceed in person to Canton, and engaged a Chinese boat at Macao for that purpose. The Chinese custom-house officer, however, refused him a permit, and bade the boatman proceed at his peril. The commodore threatened in his turn, that, unless a permit arrived by the following day, he would arm the boats of the Centurion, and proceed to Canton in defiance of the Chinese. Permission was accordingly granted. A chop for supply of provisions was obtained, and, after some delay, a farther order for laying the ship down for repair. The Centurion afterwards proceeded to sea and intercepted the valuable Acapulco, Spanish galleon, which she carried with her as a prize into the river. Duties were demanded on the Centurion and her prize. The commodore would not hear of such a demand, and repairing with his boats' crews armed to Canton, speedily obtained its relinquishment. Great delay, however, having occurred in shipping the stores, Lord Anson at last sent a letter by one of his officers to the viceroy, demanding an audience. Two days afterwards, a fire broke out in the suburbs, which was, after much destruction, got under by the efforts of the officers and seamen of the Centurion. An audience was, in consequence of this public service, granted, when the commodore availed himself of the opportunity to represent the vexatious impositions to which the British merchants were subjected, expressing his hope that the viceroy would give orders that the same should not thereafter occur. No such pledge, however, was granted. Lord Anson's conduct therefore was only successful in so far as it proved that the rule of king's ships not entering the river, was as capricious as the many other restrictions imposed upon foreigners by the local authorities, and that it might be violated with impunity. It serves also as a precedent for the proper mode of communication between an officer of the king's navy and the governor of Canton. It is remarkable that the supercargoes, influenced probably by the hong merchants, had tried to dissuade Lord Anson from seeking this interview. The merchants were then, as they still are, jealous, lest there should be any other channel than themselves of communicating with the viceroy.

In 1747, it is noted that the supercargoes, who formerly had free access to the hoppo, had been now for some years denied that privilege; so that the merchants had it in their power to practise what impositions they pleased, and to attribute them to the exactions of the mandarins.

An incident occurred at this time which, as characteristic of the local administration, is worth relating. An officer, who was about to embark from the factory, was alleged to have refused to let his escrutoire be examined by one of the hoppo's people. For this offence the linguist of the supercargoes was seized, put in chains, and the trade stopped. Though the escrutoire was afterwards inspected, and found to contain no prohibited article, and every reasonable satisfaction offered, nothing short of the officer's being delivered up to arbitrary punishment would appease the viceroy, then acting as hoppo. To this the supercargoes declared they would never consent. They desired to present a petition, and a time was fixed for its reception; but when they went, the viceroy would not see them. They were similarly disappointed a second time, but were then informed that their linguist had been released, and the affair finally settled. The non-admission to the governor's presence, notwithstanding the previous arrangement, was attributed to the merchants, by whose interference, the supercargoes alleged, the trade was placed upon such a footing, that its farther prosecution would be impracticable, unless redress were obtained. No mode, however, of gaining this object seems to have been proposed, and an excellent suggestion of the merchants themselves was neglected. It was pointed out to the supercargoes, that in 1751, the mother of the emperor would attain the age of sixty years, which is called by the Chinese the great birth-day; and which was, in the present instance, to be observed as an occasion of great rejoicing, and a proper one for the solicitation of favours. The emperor was to be at that time in the neighbourhood of Nankin; and it was suggested that some one should be sent there, with presents and a petition for a remission of the exaction of the 1950 taels, and some others which pressed on the merchants as well as on the supercargoes. So confident were the merchants of the success that would attend this step, and so much did they feel interested in the result, that they even volunteered to bear the expense of the journey and of the presents to the emperor. Mr. Misenor, who was at the time chief of the factory, declined the proposal, lest, he said, other nations should reap the benefit of his success. It does not appear that the Court of Directors dismissed Mr. Misenor with the ignominy such conduct merited; perhaps it even accorded with their own views. Their supercargoes were directed, instead of seeking admission to the emperor, to expend such a sum on the spot as they might see fit, in endeavouring to obtain relief from exactions. To an appeal to the supreme authority it would appear they were averse; and resistance to illegal extortions was a course too violent to be sanctioned by their masters at home. Bribery and corruption having less eclat than either of the other means proposed, appeared instruments better suited to the modest character of a company of merchants. The immorality probably never occurred to them, any more than the gross impolicy of feeding the very monster that was preying on the vitals of their trade. It is scarcely possible to imagine a line of conduct so pre-eminently combining meanness with folly. To satiate to its full extent the avarice of all the officers of government at Canton in succession, from time to time, would have required a far greater sacrifice than the most prosperous commerce could have repaid. But every thing that fell short of that measure of bribery, would serve only to add fuel to the flame. Whether or how far the supercargoes acted on the Court's suggestion, does not appear. Certain it is, that the wrongs they complained of, so far from being redressed, grew daily more galling. A gentleman of the name of Flint, who, having acquired a knowledge of the Chinese language, was appointed linguist to the factory, indignant at the contents of an infamous proclamation, which has continued from that time to the present to be annually repeated, and posted up against the walls of the foreign factories, drew up an address to the hoppo on the subject. This was answered by an order to the merchants to discover the writer of the address, that he might be taken up and punished, adding, "I know best what is fitting for the English."

Unable to succeed by the use of the means recommended by the Court, the supercargoes were, in 1754, forced to recur to their own measures for obtaining redress. This was to forbid the ships of the season to come up to Whampoa, till improved conditions of trade could be obtained. One of the evils complained of was the practice of requiring a merchant to be named as surety for each ship, a system which, it is remarked, had not existed above twenty years; previously to which time the supercargoes had been in the practice of themselves settling with the hoppo for the duties. The hong merchants objected to the innovation, as it tended directly to make them responsible for all duties, whether the goods were purchased by themselves or others; but principally, because it subjected them to find, at their own cost, the European curiosities by which the hoppo was accustomed to gratify his friends at Pekin, and which amounted annually to the value of 30,000 taels. It appears from the correspondence of the Select Committee of Supercargoes, that, to a period so late at least as 1811, the hoppo continued to make extortionate and constantly increasing demands on the merchants, on the same account. The superior adroitness of the native merchants in evading duties, by old weights, undervaluations and suppressions, was probably the fraudulent motive which led, in the first instance, to the voluntary transfer of responsibility from the supercargoes to the hongs; and if so, fraud, in this case,

certainly brought on its own punishment. The
supercargoes complained, that, in consequence of
this security system, merchants of credit would not
trade with them ; and alleged that they were thence
placed on a worse footing than other foreigners who
still paid their own duties. The viceroy granted
the supercargoes an audience, and instructed the
hoppo to give them, in their dealings, all the assistance in his power. The nuisance, however, was extended instead of being abated. Two persons, instead of one, were ordered to be taken as sureties for
every foreign ship, and an intimation was given, that,
in case of any deficiency in payment of the duties,
the whole body of security merchants should be
made liable for the defaulters. The hoppo farther
ordered, that the presents were, for the future, to be
at the general expense, instead of being, as formerly,
supplied by individuals incidentally, as suitable objects came into their hands. In the following year,
the monopoly of the whole foreign trade was once
more granted to the security merchants in compensation for their liabilities. This was enforced by a
prohibition on all other persons, small merchants or
shop-keepers, from engaging in it. This restriction
has never since been repealed, though it has occasionally been suffered to slumber, or to be evaded
between the privileged and unprivileged merchants.
Such temporary disuse of forbearance to enforce a
prohibition, naturally betrays some into a trap from
which, when occasion offers to revive the interdict,
they are not allowed to escape unfleeced. The pretext is always the prevention of intercourse between
traitorous natives and foreign barbarians.

E

In 1755, there occurred a case of homicide, in which an English sailor was killed by a French officer, made memorable by the extraordinary indiscretion of the English supercargoes in appealing to the Chinese authorities for redress, or rather punishment of the offender; in consequence of which an innocent Frenchman was seized and executed by the Chinese.

The hong monopoly was found to operate most injuriously on the trade, and in 1756, another ineffectual effort was made to obtain permission to deal with all merchants indiscriminately. In this endeavour, the French, Dutch, Swedish, and Prussian merchants co-operated. The influence of the hongs and the interests of the hoppo frustrated the attempt of the united foreigners. The supercargoes had to wait for seven hours before an interview could be obtained with the viceroy. In reply to their petition, they received very fair promises, which, however, were never fulfilled; and all that was in the end granted, was liberty to deal with the shopkeepers in small matters, but not for Company's exports or imports. The same exception and distinction are continued to the present day. What then becomes of the pretext of the expediency of preventing traitorous intercourse? Treason, one might think, would be as easily hatched in cheapening a watch or a piece of silk, as over a bargain for teas or broad-cloths. Falsehood is seldom consistent. One of the grounds for placing Englishmen under the tuition of their brokers or linguists, was their ignorance of the laws consequent on their ignorance of the language. A Chinese schoolmaster, however, who was at this time engaged in teach-

ing two English gentlemen, was intimidated from
farther attendance, on the ground that teaching
Europeans the language, might lead to their complaints reaching and troubling the court of Pekin.

It appears to have been about this period that
Mr. Frederick Pigou, one of the supercargoes, suggested the expediency of an embassy to Pekin.
Taking a hint from the former proposition of the
merchants to Mr. Misenor, he recommended that
the year 1761, should the empress-mother live so
long, would afford a good occasion for the mission,
as her majesty would then have attained another de-
cade of years. A still better opportunity, however,
he observed, would be offered by the accession of a
new emperor; in proof of which he cites the fact
that the ten per cent. duty had been remitted by
Keën Lung, the reigning emperor, on the occasion
of his accession. Mr. Pigou very judiciously urged,
that, instead of acting on Mr. Misenor's illiberal and
short-sighted policy, it would be both expedient in
itself, and honourable to the nation, if the same privileges and favours were procured for the merchants
of other European states as for our own. He argued
that it would, at all events, be sound policy not to
make enemies of the countrymen of the Jesuit missionaries, who enjoyed great favour at the court of
Pekin. Mr. Pigou recommended that the ambassador should be sent in the king's name; that, as now
suggested by the private merchants of Canton, he
should be a person who had never been in the Company's service, nor belonged to one of their ships;
that he should be a man of some rank and figure,—
perhaps a military man, a person of understanding

and probity, and not too haughty in his personal demeanour. The Chinese are great practical physiognomists, in the extended sense of the word, and are apt to deduce the complexion of a man's character from his general appearance. Mr. Pigou's hints are, therefore, well worthy of attention. We may add, that a full-sized figure, with a grave and commanding, yet urbane air, gives the Chinese the *beau ideal* of a great personage. Red hair they hold in abhorrence. Originally it was considered as a distinguishing trait of the Dutch; but from them the contemptuous epithet of *red-bristled* barbarians has been transferred to the English. A nervous envoy ought never to be employed on a Chinese mission; unless when failure, in order to give ground for some deep stroke of policy, is secretly desired.

Mr. Pigou adverts to the inconvenience that would result from the embassy coming to Canton; and, looking to the history of our actual missions, it is quite clear that it might have been better had they never been heard of in China till their arrival at the mouth of the Pei Ho. They failed, perhaps, from other causes; but had those not existed, the intrigues which originated at Canton, as soon as they were heard of, could not fail to have embarrassed any efforts to attain the specific objects of those embassies, relating as they did to matters chiefly affecting the interests of the provincial functionaries.

Mr. Pigou proceeds; "If more than one port was opened in China for the trade of Europeans, the mandarins would be more obliging to them than they are at Canton: for it would be a subject of emulation among them to return to court the greatest sums of money for duties; and those who used Europeans best would have the greatest number of ships come to them." A less generous motive might, perhaps, be suggested with more reason; for as the hoppo is paid by a commission on the customs, each would be impelled, by direct self-interest, to attract as much of the trade as possible to his own place of collection. "The ambassador," Mr. Pigou continues, " may solicit at court the following articles :—

1. The continuance of our privileges.
2. A remission of the duty of six per cent. imposed since the settling of the first tariff.
3. The remission of 1950 taels per ship.
4. That we be allowed the same favours and privileges in trade which the emperor's subjects enjoy, and pay no more than the emperor's stated duties on any goods exported or imported.
5. That those who deal with us, or serve us, may enjoy as much liberty as the emperor's other subjects. [At present they do not; for the mandarins force the merchants to make them presents; and the servants, that is, the linguists and compradors, to pay them money.]
6. That we may be protected by the mandarins in all cases, and particularly from the insults of the lower people.
7. That we be not made to pay duties on the import or export of our provisions, liquors, or other necessaries.
8. That effectual orders be given to prevent our goods being plundered on the river.

9. That the officers of the customs exact no presents from us.

10. That we may have leave to walk about the town, and to go from one place to another; particularly to and from Macao, without being detained by the officers of the customs, or be made to pay for our chops.

11. That access to the mandarins be made easy to us; and that the hoppo or a mandarin for that purpose be ordered to receive us at all times, and redress our grievances.

12. That we have leave to reside at Canton or elsewhere, for the better carrying on of our trade."

On our part, we should promise to "give the government no disturbance."

Mr. Pigou thought, also, that "a constant resident at the court of Pekin would be serviceable to the Company's affairs. Such a person, skilled in some science, and not meddling in matters of religion, might in time be admitted to the emperor's favour;" and if he were to marry there, and have children, he might enjoy more privileges than the missionaries do, who cannot live in their posterity; which, indeed, Mr. Pigou conceives, "is one principal reason of their making hardly any progress in the cause they have undertaken. One person settling himself thus, would soon occasion the residence of many."

Whatever may be thought of the expediency of the last of these suggestions, the rest are in strict accordance with the prayer of the Canton gentlemen in their late petition to his Majesty; at least in so far as regards the objects sought to be attained.

A curious fact is stated in this paper of Mr. Pigou, sufficiently illustrative of the necessity of having an European secretary for the Chinese language attached to any mission to the court of Pekin. "It is said that the king of Siam, in his triennial embassy to Pekin, styles himself in his letter *brother* to the emperor. His ambassador is a Siamese, but under the direction of Chinese, who make a new letter for him, wherein the king is called *tributary* to the emperor." It is remarkable that the same style from the prince regent, afterwards George the Fourth, was objected to in Lord Amherst's embassy, and an alteration acceded to : one of the many acts of vacillation which contributed to the failure of the embassy.

The Court of Directors do not appear to have approved of Mr. Pigou's plan of an embassy ; and, in fact, it was not so judicious as the former suggestion of the merchants, of a mission in the name and expressly on behalf of the Company. Mr. Ellis's reasoning seems quite applicable to the case as it then stood. As there was no treaty imposing on the Chinese any obligation as to the terms on which British subjects should be admitted to trade in the country, and as no breach of the general law of nations was complained of, nor any insult offered to the Crown through its representative, nor any attack made on the national flag, the circumstances were not such as called for interference. It is true that the arbitrary conduct of the Chinese functionaries had, in many instances, offered, at different times, good opportunities for the interposition of the British government in behalf of its subjects. Such had been the chaining of Mr. Roberts in the factory at Emoy, and the seizure and ill treatment of the officers of the Cadogan, &c. But these were unfortunately suffered to pass unnoticed, when they ought to have been taken up with spirit; and if such occasions as those were not deemed worthy of the notice of our government, it was clearly far more proper that merchants should be left to find relief from mere restrictions on their trade as they best could. Very different is the present state of circumstances. The king has been invited by the Chinese government to send out persons to control his subjects engaged in the trade with China. The request has been complied with, and the chief person bearing his Majesty's commission has been treated with insult and cruelty, accompanied by the use of terms of the most contemptuous arrogance towards our sovereign and the nation. Can these be passed over in silence? Do they not present a fitting occasion for not only humbling the presumption of this contemptible power, but of demanding that the trade be for the future so regulated, as to prevent occasions of disagreement? The propositions of Mr. Pigou, made nearly eighty years ago, are surely such as might be conceded by the Chinese, not only without any sacrifice of national advantage or dignity, but in perfect conformity with their own incessantly repeated declaration of benevolence towards foreigners; and the free merchants of the present day require no more than would have satisfied the monopolist company of 1755.

Averse to negotiate with Pekin, and finding it impossible to obtain at Canton any essential ame-

lioration of the footing on which their trade then
stood, the Court of Directors sent out instructions
to attempt again the opening of the ports of Chusan
and Ningpo to their ships. It was hoped that, as
all the local functionaries who had, twenty years
before, been guilty of such injustice and oppression
as to drive away the foreign trade from those ports,
must have been long removed, former recollections,
as far as they might be found to exist, would only
serve to make the present governor or hoppo
more cautious of giving just grounds of dissatisfaction
to their profitable visitors. A mission was accordingly sent from Canton with this view, and Mr.
Flint, who planned the mode in which it was to be
conducted, was appointed secretary and linguist.
The supercargoes were at first received in a manner
as favourable as could be desired, and every reasonable proposition for freedom of trade was acceded
to at both places. The duties were found not half
so high as at Canton. In the following year, the
supercargoes, in a letter to their successors, expressed their " hope that the trade might now be
considered as settled, although, of the twenty articles agreed to by the mandarins, several had not
been fulfilled." Excited by jealousy, intrigues were
now set on foot on the part of the authorities at Canton. The governor of Ningpo was gained over to
offer every obstruction to the trade, and 20,000 taels
paid by the mandarins and hong merchants to
officers about the court of Pekin procured an edict
from the emperor, confining the trade in future to
the single port of Canton. Upon this the governor
of Ningpo informed Mr. Flint, that he and the Eng-

lish merchants must depart immediately, for they should no longer have liberty to purchase goods, or even provisions, at that place. The unfavourable period of the monsoon was urged in vain, and Mr. Flint was forced to sea. Instead of beating to the southward, however, he bent his course to the mouth of the Pei Ho; where, by means of bribes, he succeeded in getting a petition brought to the notice of the emperor. A TA JIN, or great officer, who had been general commandant of the city of Fuh Chow Foo, the provincial capital of Fuh Keën, was, in consequence, directed to proceed to Canton, in company with Mr. Flint, to inquire into the existence of the abuses alleged in the petition. This commissioner, joined with some of the local functionaries, formed a court of inquiry on the conduct of the hoppo; and, finding that there were real grounds for the charges preferred against him, had him dismissed from office. Several impositions were taken off; but the cumsha of 1950 taels and six per cent. duties were confirmed. The emperor at the same time directed that the vessels of foreigners should no longer be termed Devil's ships, but in future be designated as Western Ocean ships. Mr. Flint's success naturally gave rise to much uneasiness in the breasts of the governor and other mandarins of Canton, who saw the danger to which they would be incessantly exposed, were a road for carrying complaints to Pekin to be left open. Unfortunately they found an opportunity of procuring at once their revenge for the past, and security for the future. Notwithstanding the imperial edict which restricted the privilege of foreign commerce to a single port, Mr. Flint was very imprudently again despatched to Ningpo. His mission failed. A representation of his contumacious disobedience was made to the emperor, and the governor of Canton obtained an order for his punishment. The following narrative, given nearly in the words of Mr. Auber, exhibits the dignified mode in which this order was announced and executed :

On the 6th December, 1759, the Tsung Tuh (viceroy) desired to see Mr. Flint, who had returned from his mission, for the purpose of communicating to the supercargoes the emperor's orders relating to the Company's affairs. The supercargoes desired to accompany him into the city, which was allowed. On arriving at the palace, the hong merchants proposed that the supercargoes should enter one by one. It is surprising that this did not excite some suspicion that injury was intended. They merely said, that as it was on the Company's affairs Mr. Flint was summoned, they must all be present. After some altercation, it was so arranged. They were received by a mandarin at the first gate, and proceeded on, through two courts, with seeming complaisance from the officers in waiting. On coming to the gate of the inner court, their swords were taken from them ; an unusual proceeding, which ought to have been construed into a symptom of danger. They were then hurried on, were forced into the presence of the Tsung Tuh, and under pretence of compelling them to pay homage after the Chinese manner, were at last thrown down. The viceroy, seeing the supercargoes resolute in their resistance to those prostrations, ordered his people to desist. He then desired Mr. Flint to advance, when he pointed to a paper which he said was the emperor's edict for his banishment to CASA-BRANCA, near Macao, for three years; at the expiration of which term, he was to return to England, never more to set foot in China. It was at the same time intimated to him that the man who had written the petition which Mr. Flint delivered at Tien Tsing, was to be beheaded that day for *treacherously encouraging such a step!* This addition to the story would be incredible elsewhere than in China; but there can be no doubt of the fact; and it has been boastingly adverted to in subsequent edicts, as instancing the great clemency with which the errors of foreigners are treated, compared with the measure of punishment awarded to those natives who are traitorously aiding and abetting in the transgression of the laws.

Mr. Flint having been thus entrapped into the hands of the viceroy, the sentence of punishment was executed upon him to its full extent. This conduct of the Chinese government was protested against by the French, Swedes, Danes, and Dutch, who represented the injustice and treachery of the whole transaction to their respective companies, who would find means of bringing the matter to the attention of the emperor; for they would not believe that if the conduct of the viceroy were made known to his majesty he would suffer it to escape punishment. A little more knowledge of China would have taught them that the viceroy could not have conducted so ticklish a business as the arrest of a barbarian in any manner that would have been more satisfactory to the emperor; inasmuch as it was effected, no matter how, without tumult. The threat was probably as much regarded as the event proved it deserved. The companies of the five nations do not appear to have taken up the matter with much warmth. The English company, indeed, so far from showing any resentment on the occasion, or complaining to the emperor as was threatened, sent a Captain Skottowe as their envoy extraordinary to the governor of Canton. This gentleman was directed to maintain his dignity by dropping the style of *Captain* and calling himself *Master;* and by falsely representing himself as brother to his majesty's private secretary.

The court, in their address to the viceroy, began by expressing their mortification at being excluded from Ningpo, as if their mortification were not his triumph, and as if that measure had not emanated from the emperor himself, or could have been repealed by the governor of Canton if he would. They proceeded to request the liberation of Mr. Flint; the remission of the 1950 taels; the six per cent. on all imports, and of the two per cent. on silver paid to the hoppo—all matters that had received the imperial sanction. They further requested to be allowed to pay as formerly their own duties; that the hoppo should be directed always to hear the representations of the supercargoes; and that they might appeal direct to the governor.

This imbecile address was accompanied by equally imbecile instructions to the supercargoes to pay *constant attention* to the hong confederacy, which had now been for two years in full vigour, and in all their proceedings to adopt only pacific and conciliatory measures.

The governor of Canton stated, in reply to the

East India Company, that " every year when the foreign ships enter the port, the hoppo ought, by law, to go to Whampoa and superintend the measurement of the ships : and that also, by regulation, he makes presents of cattle to foreigners five or six times a-year. At such times all the foreigners are present; and if they have any affairs about which they require to present a petition, can embrace those opportunities of doing so. But indeed the hoppo does not refuse permission to any foreign merchant to appear before him. Hereafter, should there be any really important case, which cannot be deferred till an opportunity when the measurement takes place, it is permitted to the said foreigners to go themselves in company with a security merchant and a linguist to the hoppo's office, and there present their petition. Nor are the officers in charge of the gates allowed from selfish motives, to prevent their entrance." The hoppo has in fact long since ceased to visit the shipping at Whampoa; and the condition of being accompanied by a security merchant and a linguist, rendered the permission to petition him in person at other times nearly nugatory; as the subject matter of complaint was generally the conduct of those very merchants and linguists.

As far as regarded Mr. Flint, a more offensive mode was pursued. The governor and Foo Yuen addressed a letter to his Britannic Majesty, in which they informed him " that in the mere imprisonment of Mr. Flint, it is not that criminal alone, who has received such amazingly gracious treatment that he should think of it with tears, and should rouse up all his grateful feelings; but likewise all the foreigners

of his nation have been so drenched with the waves
of the imperial favour, that they should leap for joy,
and turn towards us for civilization!" They go on
to say, in the style of command "We make it clearly
known to the king of the said nation, that he forthwith, acting in obedience to this precept, may take
Mr. Flint and order him to be kept in safe custody
and restrained."

There can be no doubt that the government of
China had a perfect right to interdict Mr. Flint from
returning to Ningpo. But there was no law of the
country by which Mr. Flint had subjected himself
to imprisonment; far less to any more severe punishment as hinted at by the governor of Canton and
Foo Yuen. And though absolute and perpetual expulsion from the country would have been quite
within the scope of the natural authority of its sovereign with respect to any stranger who had disobeyed
his ordinances, by no reasonable construction of international law could a foreigner be deemed amenable
to arbitrary punishment for an offence such as Mr.
Flint's, that involved in its commission no injury
whatever either to individuals or to the state. His
three years' imprisonment formed therefore a case of
wrong, which might have been taken up by our
government as an occasion of temperate remonstrance.
It would have been no difficult matter to have made
such a man as Keën Lung sensible that his officers
had, through their ignorance, committed a great mistake, in presuming to address an independent sovereign in the style which they had adopted; and that
the expulsion of Mr. Flint from China, by which he
was deprived of the means of subsistence, would have

been an adequate punishment. The emperor might have been, at the same time, assured, that observance of the laws was strictly enjoined on all British subjects visiting China; so that, if his imperial majesty should at any future time deem it expedient to admit their commerce at other ports than Canton, their conduct would be found to be perfectly orderly and inoffensive. Such a communication might have gradually led to a treaty of commerce, which would at least have placed the trade on a more secure footing than it has ever yet enjoyed. Nothing that had at that time occurred had begun to excite alarm or jealousy among the Chinese, and the conduct of the English in commercial matters was above reproach. No farther notice, however, was taken of Mr. Flint's wrongs, and the insult offered to the king of England was submitted to in silence; or more probably it was never brought to the notice of his majesty's government.

This passiveness appears to have paved the way for fresh indignities; for in 1765, when the hoppo insisted upon measuring a king's ship, called the Argo, the supercargoes, who objected, offered at the same time to pay for her the same amount of duty as was payable for the largest of the Company's ships. After such an offer it was in vain to plead the precedent of Lord Anson's ship. The hoppo shrewdly asked what they meant by offering to pay measurage in lieu of letting the ship be measured; adding, that if it was not submitted to, the supercargoes must leave the country, and the merchants be bambooed and sent into banishment. This was the first occasion on which such a threat had been resorted to, and its use was the direct consequence of our exclusion from other ports. Previously to the adoption of that measure by the Chinese, it was we who used to threaten to quit the port of Canton, —not they to turn us out; we, who to a certain extent, prescribed the conditions on which we would consent to trade,—not they the terms on which we should be permitted to do so. After four months' discussion, his majesty's frigate was treated as a common merchant ship and was measured! With the experience of half a century of the high value set by the Chinese, by the court itself, and particularly by the local government on the foreign trade, those weak men acted as if they believed the hoppo either meant or dared to have acted up to his threats. Unfortunately for the honour of his majesty's navy and their own future embarrassments, their foolish fears were augmented by the indecision of the commander of the Argo. The viceroy alleged, when appealed to, that Lord Anson escaped measurement because he had come into the river in distress; choosing to forget that, on his second arrival, he came not in distress, but bringing with him a rich prize to Whampoa. In 1771, the cohong, or regulating committee, for fixing the prices at which all goods should be bought and sold, was abolished by the viceroy. This order was obtained at the cost of 100,000 taels, paid by a hong merchant on account of the Company, who made good the money. It is exceedingly improbable that a hong merchant would have taken any trouble to procure the abolition of an institution from the existence of which he was deriving advantage. The most natural con-

F

clusion, therefore, is, that the merchants, finding the rules of the cohong injurious or inconvenient to themselves, for whose benefit and at whose instance it had been established, and desirous of ridding themselves of the mandarins who claimed a share in their profits, were themselves desirous of the abolition of the association; and that they procured its dissolution as a matter of course, without having any occasion to resort to bribery to effect it. If so, corruption in this case over-reached itself.

In 1773 occurred the first of the cases, already alluded to, of the judicial murder of a foreigner by the Chinese. A native had been murdered at Macao, and suspicion fell on an Englishman named Thomas Scott. The accused was examined and depositions taken, but not a trace of evidence was found against Scott. The mandarins, however, threatened the city, unless the party who had been suspected was given up to them. Some members of the Portuguese senate urged that it would be unjustifiable to consent to the sacrifice of an innocent man ; but these were over-ruled by the holy vicar-general, who prevailed on the majority to adopt the principle, that the life of an individual, however in; nocent, was not to be weighed against the safety of the state. Honour and conscience were disregarded in the estimate of the man of God and his friends. Scott was given up and executed.

In 1780, a Frenchman who had in a fray killed another sailor, a Portuguese, was, after some hesitation, given over to the mandarins by the French consul, and was, forthwith, without any formal trial, strangled by order of the Foo Yuen.

It appears also that in 1762, a Dutch sailor who
had killed his comrade was left by the mandarins to
be punished by his own countrymen; so that the
general principle might have been considered as
well established. In the year 1784 the evil example of the Macao
government and of the French consul was followed
by the English supercargoes, under circumstances
still less pardonable. With such recent examples
before them of the utter disregard of the Chinese
functionaries of either the substance or semblance
of justice, they delivered up to them the gunner of
the Lady Hughes, who, in firing a salute, was accidentally the cause of the death of a Chinese. The
conduct of the mandarins was, in this instance,
marked by the usual stamp of cowardice, treachery,
and cruelty. After repeated conferences between
the English and Chinese, the latter declared themselves satisfied that the fatal event was purely accidental, and the affair was supposed to be set finally
at rest. Notwithstanding this, on the morning after
the last conference, the supercargo of the ship was,
while attending to his business, decoyed away, and
conveyed into the city under a guard, and there
held in confinement. This outrage spread general
alarm amongst the foreigners at Canton, insomuch
that the supercargoes at the suggestion of the other
merchants, ordered up the boats of the several ships
manned and armed, to guard the factory. Similar
measures were adopted by the French, Dutch,
Danes, and Americans. In their passage up the
river, one of the boats was fired upon and a man
was wounded, but no step was taken to obtain repa-

ration for this act of direct hostility. Seeing this, the Chinese still refused to deliver up the supercargo till the gunner of the Lady Hughes should be surrendered to them. While the foreigners remained shamefully inactive, the troops of the province were called in; Chinese servants were withdrawn; all intercourse was at an end; and the naval force was increased: every thing, in fact, showed their expectation of war. They meant to intimidate, but certainly would have yielded rather than have suffered matters to go to such an extremity. They artfully managed to detach the other foreigners from the English by restoring their trade, and declaring that if the gunner were given up it was their intention that he should have an impartial trial; and if it appeared that the death of the Chinese was purely accidental, he should be released unhurt. The supercargoes, alarmed at this defection, and relying on the promise of the Foo Yuen, gave the man up; when they were again assured by the mandarins that they need be under no uneasiness as to his fate. In a few weeks afterwards the unfortunate and innocent gunner was strangled. On the occasion of declaring the sentence, the mercantile gentlemen of the different nations were summoned to attend the mandarins, and were informed by them, " that the emperor was greatly displeased at their having so long delayed giving the man up; and observed that the government had been extremely moderate in demanding the life of one foreigner for the lives of two of their subjects who had been killed by the accident." This aggravation of circumstances would justify the suspicion that the whole had been misrepresented to the emperor, were we not aware that his decision would have been the same in any case. A purely accidental homicide by a native, is punished by a small fine payable to the relatives of the deceased. The Court of Directors, in commenting upon this case, expressed sentiments to much the same effect, though not so plainly spoken, as those of the pious vicargeneral of Macao. The emperor himself could not have intimated more strongly his displeasure at the delay in delivering up the victim ; and while every honest Englishman's face to this very day, tingles with shame at the recital of the cowardly inactivity that suffered the supercargo of the Lady Hughes to remain a prisoner at Canton while there was a force on the spot sufficient to have sacked the place, the Court of Directors are angry that their servants should have run the risk of displeasing the Chinese by taking a measure which they thought necessary for their own personal security. Much of the contumely and oppression, to which foreigners have been since subjected, may be fairly traced to their contemptible submissiveness in this instance. Others might be pardoned for distrusting their own force, but the countrymen of Weddell and of Anson had no such apology for their pusillanimous conduct. In justice to the Court of Directors, however, it should be stated, that they generously authorised a resort to bribery on future similar occasions, in order to obtain favourable reports of the cases from the judicial authorities.

The Consoo Fund, which has subsequently pressed so severely on the trade, had its origin in 1782.

The Company's supercargoes being unwilling or unable to afford aid in the recovery of certain claims due to some British merchants at Madras, who appear to have had influence with that government, these obtained, from Lord Macartney, a recommendation of their claims to the protection of the admiral on the station. His excellency accordingly despatched Captain Panton of the Sea-Horse frigate with a letter to the governor of Canton, demanding that justice should be done to his majesty's subjects. An interview, as insisted upon, was obtained, though after some delay, and not without recourse being had to threats. Had the viceroy persevered, Captain Panton would probably have followed the example of the Ann, and helped himself to indemnity on account of the clients whose cause he had come to plead, by the seizure of a sufficient number of Chinese junks. A reference was made to the emperor, who directed that the debts should be paid by the whole of the hong merchants jointly. They were, at the same time, prohibited from incurring debts to foreigners for the future; and certain mandarins were appointed through whom all their transactions with foreigners were to be conducted. This led to the renewal of the cohong, for the abolition of which 100,000 taels had been paid a few years before. The cohong resolved upon re-imbursing themselves the amount which the emperor's edict had compelled them to pay by the imposition of a tax on teas, and on a variety of imports which necessarily passed through their hands. Debts, and those for very large sums, continued, notwithstanding the emperor's edict, to be incurred by the hong merchants; and when they at last became bankrupt, it was out of this tax on the trade that those debts were discharged. The last payment that could be claimed on this account from the Consoo Fund has been made some time ago, but this unauthorised tax is still maintained, while the grounds of its original imposition no longer exist. No debts incurred by a hong merchant subsequently to March 1830, can fall upon the cohong; but it is from this source that all the funds are still raised out of which the demands of the mandarins are satisfied.

The above-mentioned interference on the part of a British admiral affords a second instance of direct communication between a naval officer and the viceroy of Canton.

Emboldened by the apparent impotence of the supercargoes to protect either themselves or their countrymen from injustice, the most vexatious duties were levied even upon the provisions required for their use. The Bellona, which had been one year obliged, through the Company's servants, acting under compulsion, to pay duties as on a full freight, though she took away none, was, on her next voyage, forced to dispose of her cargo to a particular merchant pointed out by the hoppo. Every attempt at remonstrance against such impositions as these was sure to bring on a suspension of the trade. In this most unpleasant manner matters went on for some years, when, in 1789, an opportunity offered of a nature similar to that which had presented itself to Mr. Misenor in 1751, and to those other opportunities of which Mr. Pigou had suggested that advantage should be taken to send a deputation to

Pekin. It was proposed by the hoppo of that
period that a mission should be sent on behalf of the
Company to congratulate the emperor on the attainment of his eightieth year. Had this invitation been
acted upon by men of ordinary intelligence and
address, the way might have been opened for placing the whole of our commercial relations with
China on a new and improved footing. But it was
unhappily declined; partly from an alleged apprehension of the personal insecurity that would attend
the journey, and partly from an unwillingness to
submit to the ceremonials which would be required
on the occasion of presentation to the emperor.
Objections more futile, or more indicative of the
total want of vigour and capacity which characterised
the select committees of those days, cannot well be
imagined. On their journey the commissioners,
proceeding as they could only have done under the
imperial sanction, would, of course, have enjoyed the
protection of the government. As to conventional
forms of ceremony, they are nothing in themselves;
and however objectionable, or rather inadmissible,
would be the performance of any act whatever, that
implied an acknowledgment of dependence on the
emperor of China, if required from a representative of
the British monarch, it could be no degradation to
the servants of a mercantile company, engaged in a
trade carried on under the protection of the Chinese
government, to pay the same marks of respect to its
head as are shown by subjects of the highest rank in
the empire. Those gentlemen unfortunately held
their dignity to be less compromised by remaining
subject to constantly reiterated threats of being

made personally responsible for the conduct of persons over whom they could exercise little or no control ; while their employers were, from time to time, subjected to heavy losses by suspensions of the trade, a measure which came to be commonly resorted to by the mandarins, " aware," as the supercargoes themselves state, " that the importance attached by us to its continuance, inclines us to submit to almost every indignity."

In 1791, one of their number expressed his opinion that " great advantages might be drawn from the trade with China, if an ill-founded apprehension of its loss did not deter us from urging pretensions to such privileges as would make our commerce with the country safe and honourable, which I am sorry to say it is not."

The Court of Directors, however, seem to have been wedded to the spirit of quietism in China ; so that when, in 1792, the late Lord Melville, then Mr. Dundas, who was at the head of the Board of Control, proposed to send an embassy to Pekin, they evinced no disposition to encourage the project, expressing great doubts as to the probability of any advantage arising from the measure. Mr. Dundas, however, had a clear perception of the disadvantage of having no other port than Canton open to the trade ; of having, even there, the fair competition of the market destroyed by the monopoly of the hongs; of the denial to British subjects of free access to the tribunals of the country ; and of the arbitrary state of depression under which they were kept by the local authorities,—a depression scarcely compatible with the regulations of civilized society, and therefore thought the experiment of an embassy for the removal of those evils well worth trying. Unfortunately, as if any doubt could have existed of the venality and corruption in which all those evils had had their origin, instead of making the extirpation of that canker the primary and immediate object of the embassy, it was proposed, as a question to be solved, whether those evils did not proceed out of some settled policy of the Imperial government, founded, perhaps, on its jealousy of the national character; as if all other foreigners were not, at least, as ill treated as the English. Had they, on the contrary, set out with a clear and strong representation of the habitual extortions and unauthorised exactions of the local functionaries, which Keën Lung could have no desire nor motive to support or defend,—and (when these allegations had been once established to the conviction of the monarch) proceeded to a review of those measures which had been recommended to his majesty by interested persons, under some plausible pretext of public expediency,—it is not unlikely that, his eyes being once opened to the injustice and impolicy into which he had been betrayed, all the evils complained of might have been removed. But, this order of proceeding being inverted, it was easy for any one who had access to the emperor, to poison his ears against foreigners, and to persuade him that he ought not, for their convenience or gratification, to depart from resolutions regarding the trade which his wisdom had deemed it expedient to adopt. It should have been recollected that the monarch to whom the embassy was sent was the same man who, after punishing his own officers for their misdeeds towards foreigners, had also inflicted chastisement on Mr. Flint for disregard to his edicts; though, from the candour of his character, he would just as certainly have revoked the prohibition from trading to Chusan, had the impure motives of those who had recommended that measure to him been made apparent.

One great disadvantage under which Lord Macartney's embassy laboured, was ignorance of the court to which it was addressed. Intrigues were on foot to oppose the objects of the mission, which, from want of knowledge of the characters and connections of the parties, it was impossible to neutralize or to counteract. Had Lord Macartney been aware of the excessive corruption and venality of Ho Kwan, the prime minister and all-influential favourite, it might have been easy for him to have shaken the unlimited confidence reposed in that minister by the emperor, as may be inferred from the following anecdote : " Having suspected him of a falsehood, he degraded him at once, but with that love of justice which formed the best trait in the character of Keën Lung, he restored him to his rank and offices the moment he discovered his suspicions had been unjust." The immense riches which Ho Kwan had amassed could be no secret, and the powerful temptation they offered to Imperial cupidity proved his ruin. Immediately after his master's death, he was put on his trial by Kea King, found guilty of course, his enormous property confiscated, and himself put to death.

It was another misfortune or error in the conduct of this embassy, that its objects were allowed to transpire, and were divulged at Macao and Canton, before the arrival of the ships that conveyed it to the coast of China. This gave opportunity and leisure for those parties that were interested in its failure to set to work every engine that could promote such a result. The hoppo had particular reasons for apprehension on the occasion, and his zeal and activity were roused to proportionate exertion, in exciting his friends at the imperial palace to undermine the ambassador. We find this very hoppo, under the name of Soo Ta Jin, afterwards holding a conspicuous situation in the reception of Lord Amherst's embassy. There can be no doubt, therefore, that he was, while hoppo, and that he continued to be afterwards, a man of considerable court influence. In fact, as the appointment is reckoned worth from two to three hundred thousand taels a year (60,000*l.* to 100,000*l.*), it is only bestowed on court favourites, and its emoluments enable the possessor to maintain the influence that placed him in the situation. The embassy of Lord Macartney was not, however, absolutely without any beneficial results. The old emperor was personally gratified by the mission, and it was a most extraordinary mistake on the part of the Directors, and of the king's ministers, that they did not avail themselves of an invitation to renew the intercourse in 1796, on the occasion of the emperor's attaining the 60th year of his reign. A knowledge of the sovereign and of the court had been attained, on the first visit, that would have been of infinite advantage to a mission so speedily following it; while, the performance of the *Ko-tow* having been dispensed with in that instance, an exemption from the ceremony being conceded a second time would for ever have placed the national dignity on a higher footing, in the eyes of the whole empire, than that of any other country that had sent an embassy to China. The occasion itself, too, would have been peculiarly favourable for soliciting concessions.

It was unfortunate that the permission granted to the Hindostan (the vessel that conveyed the presents) to load, if desired at Chusan, was not availed of. The local authorities there would, perhaps, have attempted exactions of an unauthorised description; and if so, an occasion for complaint direct to the emperor would have been afforded, with which the extortions of the mandarins of Canton might have been incidentally introduced. On the other hand, if, in deference to the Imperial authority, no illegal demands were made at Chusan, the contrast with the conduct of the authorities at the other port would have served as good grounds for soliciting attention to their injustice and impositions.

On the return of the Lion, after landing the embassy at the Pei Ho, she waited at Whampoa for the arrival of the embassy from Pekin; nor does it appear that any objection was made to her admission within the forts of the Bogue, on account of her being a ship of war.

It was most lamentable that, on this first occasion of intercourse between the monarchs of Great Britain and China, the embassy was unprovided with an English secretary well skilled in the Chinese language. Had this been done, Lord Macartney would never have been betrayed, as he was, into any form of language implying that his country was tributary to the Celestial empire. Or, had the designation of tribute-bearer been submitted to as a mere matter of usage, he would have taken care to have had a formal document to that effect placed in his hands. It is now alleged that, in one of his addresses to the emperor, his interpreter headed the paper as the petition of the " Red-bristled Barbarian Tribute-bearer." In China, as has been most justly remarked, words and ceremonies are things. They are classed amongst the essentials fully as much as they have ever been in Europe. " The Barbarians," says a Chinese author of repute, " cannot be governed in the same way as the middle kingdom (China) is ruled. They are like brutes, and therefore to them the great principles of government must be productive of much anarchy. The former kings knew this, and therefore they ruled over them by misrule. To govern them by misrule is the way to rule them completely." According to the late Dr. Morrison, the spirit of the 225th section of the Leu Lee, or Penal Laws of China, is that all barbarians are ene-mies to China — that she allows no free nor friendly intercourse with other countries — that she wishes to keep her affairs secret from foreigners — that all, except such as are licensed by government, who trade with foreigners are traitors. If any are at all suspected of giving information, legal advice, or simi-lar aid, to a foreigner, the local government imme-diately raises the cry of traitor ! Those natives who teach the language to foreigners, or write a petition for them, or show a foreigner the way to the city-gate of Canton, that he may there present a petition, are designated and punishable as such. The punishment is, in some cases, as in that of Mr. Flint's translator, death by decapitation. The word *Man* conveys, in common speech, the sense of rude, cruel, savage, and is commonly joined to the word *Ee,* signifying savage barbarians, which is often heard applied to European gentlemen. Were this a question of mere philology, it would not be incurious; but the ideas cherished and perpetuated by such language are pernicious to the welfare of mankind, because they generate in weak and ignorant minds reciprocal animosity. The Greeks and Romans not only gave the degrading appellation of Barbarians to every other people, but, in consequence, asserted a right of domination over them, as the soul has over the body, and men have over irrational animals. Aristotle advised Alexander to treat the Greeks as subjects, and the barbarians as slaves; to rule them by misrule. And, in more modern times, we know how the Christians of Europe have treated the people they deemed barbarians and savages. Etymology fixes not the meaning of any word. Use is the law of signification; and *Man ee,* in the Chinese sense, means a man uncivilised or untaught, perhaps one cruel and savage. Such was the opinion of one of the first Chinese scholars of our times, and it is therefore certainly not to be lightly treated or disregarded. Before the rise of the present dynasty, the Tartars were classed under one denomination of barbarians, as Teih, or Fiery Dogs. What Chinese dares now apply to them that designation? It would not be difficult for a classical sinalogue like Mr.

Gutzlaff, to demonstrate to the Chinese themselves, that the English nation cannot, with propriety, be included amongst any of the four classes of Barbarians alluded to by ancient writers. In the meantime, however, they are so classed, and they submit to it : and must, therefore, so long as they do so, expect to be subjected to the prescribed mode of treatment—to be ruled by misrule. It is true that, when hard pressed by a proficient in the language, the Chinese functionaries hesitate not to disclaim the intention of conveying any derogatory idea of foreigners by the appellations alluded to, yet they most pertinaciously adhere to their use in preference to other words that simply express the English term foreigners. It is, however, because foreigners are barbarians, that, according to Chung the hoppo, hong merchants and linguists are appointed to *repress their pride and profligacy.* " The *Hwa* and *Ee*, the *flowery* natives and the barbarians, must be distinctly divided." It would be tedious to trace the operation of this principle through all its ramifications of denial of justice, commercial restrictions, and personal insult and privation. Enough has been said to show that all those evils have their root in the degradation of those who are subjected to them. Eradicate this false estimation ; and injurious treatment, having no longer any principle to support it, must fall to the ground of itself.

But to return from this digression. Instead of waiting till 1796, letters, accompanied with presents from the king of England to the emperor of China, and from Lord Macartney, Mr. Dundas, Sir George Staunton, the chairman and deputy-chairman of

the Court of Directors to the viceroy and hoppo
of Canton, were transmitted in 1795, apparently
with no specific object. The presents to the emperor were accepted, but the viceroy and hoppo
declined those intended for them, on the alleged
ground that they were addressed to their predecessors in office. The advantages derived from the
embassy and those presents, as enumerated by the
supercargoes in 1799, were certainly not very striking. They were " a general diminution in the ex-
penses of the supercargoes' removal to and from
Canton ; the cessation of interference on the part
of the mandarins in the allotment to the several
hong merchants of the Company's business, and an
abstinence from the habitual resort, as a measure of
coercion, to the suspension of the trade." The consoo fund, out of which all general exactions on the
merchants were to be defrayed, still remained a
burden on commerce. Goods continued to be unfairly weighed by the hoppo ; and the country ships
to be unfairly measured ; undue charges were made
on the transfer of stores from ship to ship at Whampoa ; and the exorbitant fees on shipping remained
as before.

In 1799 Captain Dilkes, of H. M. ship Madras,
refused to give up a man who had wounded a Chinese in a boat, in an attempt to steal. Another
Chinese had at the same time thrown himself overboard from the boat, and was drowned. The supercargoes were threatened, but Captain Dilkes having
left the river, the matter was dropped. The wounded
native recovered, and acknowledged that the man

G

who was drowned had gone overboard of his own accord.

In 1801, the Select Committee applied to the viceroy for a copy of the laws of China; this was refused on the plea of their being exceedingly voluminous, but a few articles by way of extracts were furnished to them, in which the punishment of accidental homicide is said to be according to the law of blows given in an affray; but it is not stated what that law is : it is probable that the truth could not have been told without a virtual acknowledgment that the execution of the gunner of the Lady Hughes had been a judicial murder. In the same year an attempt was alleged by the Chinese to have been made, by some persons belonging to a Company's ship, to smuggle a few camlets on shore. This was made a pretext for fining the hong merchant who was security for the ship in the sum of 50,000 taels, upwards of 16,000*l.*

Notwithstanding the refusal of the viceroy and hoppo in 1799 to accept the presents that were sent to them from England, it was resolved by his majesty's government that the experiment should be repeated, and that the English prime minister should on the same occasion address the prime minister at Pekin, also with presents, " with a view to conciliate him to British interests," in other words, to bribe him. The viceroy and hoppo declined their presents as before; but on the new plea " that the invariable practice and general laws of the empire prevented any officer of government from receiving letters or presents from the ministers or mandarins of foreign nations." That the same objection did not apply to receiving presents from foreign merchants was pretty well known to the supercargoes, who stated the expense they were put to on occasions of admission to an audience by the viceroy, as one of the grounds of their unwillingness to resort frequently to that measure when seeking redress of injuries. In reply to the letter addressed to the emperor, his majesty was graciously pleased to express his approbation of the king of England's *observance* of *duty* and *obedience;* adding, that as the celestial government regards all persons with eyes of charity and benevolence, and always treats British subjects with the utmost indulgence and affection, there can be no plea nor occasion for the exertions of their own government on their behalf. KEEN LUNG resigned the crown in the 60th year of his reign, and the trembling jealous despot KEA KING was the emperor with whom this flattering and gratifying correspondence took place. It was not thought necessary to require that the imperial secretaries should be called to account for the insolent pretension of addressing the king of England as a vassal. Conciliation was the order of the day; and it would appear as if the administration cared little at what expense of national dignity that object was attained.

Fortunately a better spirit animated some officers both of the Company's service and of his majesty's navy. In 1807 some of the crew of a Company's ship on leave at Canton fell into a drunken quarrel with some Chinese. Their commander succeeded in getting them into the factory; but the Chinese having followed them in great numbers, continued throughout the day to throw stones at the factory, and at every European passing, although mandarins and security merchants were present, and called out to the mob to disperse. At last the sailors, provoked beyond endurance, made a sally on the Chinese, and unfortunately killed one man before they could be brought back. The Select Committee of Super-cargoes endeavoured, but unsuccessfully, to get the matter hushed up. The surrender of Sheen, the individual who had been supposed guilty of the homicide, was insisted upon; but where so many were engaged, it was impossible to discover which had actually struck the fatal blow. Of this the mandarins could not fail to be sensible, as they themselves conducted an inquiry into the matter at the Company's factory. The trade was stopped for two months, but the supercargoes, supported by Captain Rolles, of H. M. ship Lion, having resolutely refused to give up to the Chinese the man who was alleged to have been most active in the affray, a false story, utterly wide of the facts of the case, was got up by the mandarins and reported to Pekin, in consequence of which the trade was re-opened and the man suffered to be released. This result, it is said, was obtained at the expense of about 50,000*l.* in bribes to the officers of justice and relations of the deceased. At one part of the investigation, it seems, a most treacherous attempt was made to seize Sheen's person, in violation of the most positive stipulations in writing to the contrary. The whole of these proceedings received the approbation of the Court of Directors. Captain Rolles was presented by them with 1000*l.* for his services on this occasion. It did not occur to the Court, that the immensity of the bribes that had been resorted to, might operate as a premium for bringing their supercargoes into trouble as often as similar opportunities could be found for doing so. At the same time, the determined resistance of Captain Rolles, and even the pecuniary sacrifices submitted to by the supercargoes, went far to redeem the national disgrace that had been incurred by the abandonment of the unfortunate gunner of the Lady Hughes, by whose innocent blood, it has been justly remarked, the Company's servants of the day purchased the continuance of their commerce.

A fatal mistake was committed in 1808 by the occupation of Macao, without the previous sanction of either the Portuguese or Chinese authorities, or provision regarding the line of conduct to be adopted in case of the determined opposition of either party to that measure. This step was taken by the Bengal government at the suggestion of the Committee of Supercargoes, lest the French should be beforehand with us. It did not seem to be known either to the supercargoes, or to the Bengal government, that the Portuguese hold Macao, not as a free colony, but merely as tenants of the Chinese government, paying annual rent for the ground they occupy, and admitting Chinese jurisdiction to a great extent over the settlement. Had the French, indeed, acted in the manner apprehended, nothing would have been more easy than their expulsion by the co-operation of the English with the Chinese, and we might have attached our own terms to our assistance on the occasion. It is not even improbable that, had such an event taken place, the Chinese might

have assented to our retaining possession of the
place on terms of greater independence of Chinese
authority than those on which it is held by
the Portuguese. Even then, if such a grant were
to be coupled, as it very probably would be, with
the interdict against trading at Canton, under which
the Portuguese themselves lie, the expediency of
accepting it would be very doubtful. From their
subsequent proceedings, however, the supercargoes
would appear to have thought the possession of
Macao an object of importance, even though held in
defiance of the Chinese, as if the latter, by inter-
dicting commerce, and even supplies of provisions to
Macao, could not render such a settlement useless,
or even untenable, whenever they chose. Much
bullying took place on both sides, but at length
Admiral Drury, who commanded the expedition,
having declared that his instructions did not prevent
his going to war with China, an edict of the emperor
on the subject was availed of as a pretext for withdrawing the troops ; a result which was, of course,
triumphantly attributed by the viceroy of Canton, and
universally so by the people, to our dread of Chinese
prowess. In consequence of this demonstration of
military force on the part of the English, the emperor
directed that in future no vessels should be permitted to go to Whampoa till a reference had been
made to Pekin for permission. The fears which had
dictated this precaution subsiding, while the inconvenience to both parties was found to be very great,
the order was a few months afterwards repealed.
So much for the immutability of imperial regulations.
   The disapprobation of the Court of Directors of the

conduct of their supercargoes, in not at once yielding
to the mandates of the local government, was marked
by their removal of the Select Committee from their
situations. Undoubtedly the Court was right. If
it was deemed expedient to occupy Macao in spite
of the Chinese, the British force ought, on receipt of
the first threat from the Canton government, to have
proceeded to the provincial capital, and there dictated
their own terms. Unless the cause was such as
would justify proceeding to that extremity, friendly
negotiation alone was admissible.

On this occasion, a seventy-four and two frigates
passed within the Bogue. According to the evidence
of Mr. Marjoribanks before a Committee of Parliament, Admiral Drury went in person to Canton, and
there sent an intimation to the viceroy that he would
be at his palace in the city in half an hour. The
viceroy declined so abrupt a visit, and Admiral
Drury quietly returned to his ship. He afterwards
armed his boats with the avowed intention of break-
ing through a line of Chinese boats placed to inter-
cept his passage to the city. He was fired upon—
one of his men wounded—and he desisted from the
attack. These attempts ought never to have been
made, or they should have been persisted in till the
end desired was accomplished. There is nothing so
necessary, in dealing with the Chinese, as keeping
the ground once assumed.

In 1810, another case of homicide occurred. An
investigation into the circumstances was conducted
in the Company's factory by the mandarins, and
though no evidence was adduced to throw suspicions
on any party, the ships which were ready to depart

were refused their grand chop, or pass, till some individual should be given up for punishment. It was, however, intimated to the hoppo, that unless passes were granted by a given day, the ships would depart without them; and they were actually on their way to the mouth of the river, when passes were granted, on a promise that the matter should be inquired into in England, and the offenders, when discovered, punished. The Court of Directors were pleased to express their dissatisfaction with these proceedings. It does not appear that bribery had been resorted to on the occasion; and the super-cargoes had refused to answer the requisition of the government in terms which were suggested, " because those were both false in fact, and danger-ous in principle, and, further, disgraceful by the implication of promises never intended or expected to be performed." It is not to be presumed that these peculiarities of the case formed the grounds of the offence taken by the honourable Court, though we are left at a loss to conjecture what they really were. On a reference to the Privy Council, it was declared that in the existing state of the law, the men who were suspected to be guilty could not be brought to trial in England; but no steps were taken to have this gross defect in the laws remedied. Had the guilty parties in this instance been detected, and brought to due punishment, we should never again have had difficulties in coming to an arrangement with the Chinese in cases of homicide.

The southern coasts of China had been for some years infested by pirates, who proved themselves greatly an overmatch for the Chinese navy. The local authorities invited the Portuguese to their assistance, which was afforded on condition of a certain stipulated payment, and a vague promise of being restored to their ancient immunities. Though some British subjects, who had been seized in an open boat, were at that time prisoners in the piratical fleet, the supercargoes do not seem to have made use of the large force of Indiamen at their command, sufficient as that was to have destroyed the whole piratical power in a few days, but sent to Bengal for aid, and in the meantime contented themselves with furnishing the Portuguese vessels employed with such stores as they required. After all, the Chinese found it expedient to come to terms with the pirates, granting the leaders abundant favours and amends for their submission, and to their followers an absolute amnesty. Such is the manner in which insurrections are usually quelled by this overbearing but impotent and dastardly government. When the service was over, the Portuguese were told that they still possessed all the privileges they had ever enjoyed, and that they had therefore nothing to claim under the engagement of restoring them to their ancient immunities ; an assertion contradicted by the whole tenor of the early records of Macao.

Several interruptions occurred in the progress of loading the ships of the season 1810-11. The hong merchants, on being remonstrated with, were unanimous in acknowledging that the detention was a measure of the local government, directed against themselves, in consequence of the absolute inability of most of them, and the actual refusal of all to satisfy the extortionate and continually increasing demands of the hoppo for the purchase of various articles of clock-work and mechanism imported by officers of the Company's ships, and which it seemed had become the established vehicle of corruption between that personage and his superiors of the capital. Instead of letting corruption take its course, which would probably have terminated in the ruin of the hong merchants, and the exposure of its cause, the supercargoes appear to have lost sight of all the relief to their commerce that they might expect from the destruction of the system of which they had so long, so loudly, and so justly complained. They suggested that the shipment of such articles should be prohibited for the future ; as if there were but one class of objects suited to the purpose, and with the failure of a supply of these articles, exactions on the part of the hoppo would cease.

But though it would have been good policy to let the whole body of hong merchants fall into a state of insolvency, it is true that a partial bankruptcy would, in the first instance at least, serve only to render more powerful the monopoly of the remainder,—a view of the subject which led the supercargoes to lend most active support to those of the number that were on the eve of being treated as bankrupts by the government. It appears that, so far back as 1806, at least one-half of the hong merchants were in a state of insolvency; had they been declared bankrupts, their property would have been confiscated to government ; the leading partners would have been banished to ELEE, in Tartary, and the payment of their debts would have been thrown on the remaining merchants, to be discharged by them out of the consoo fund, or, in other words, by a further tax on commerce. It did not apparently occur to the supercargoes, or to the Court of Directors, that, by stopping the trade on the plausible ground of such a state of things being incompatible with its advantageous continuance, and insisting, on the payment by the government of the money due to them by the hongs, they would have placed the local authorities in a situation of the greatest embarrassment, from which they probably would have been too happy to be able to extricate themselves by restoring the trade to its original free footing. There was quite time enough for deliberation, as well as for effecting the desired purpose, without any heavy loss. The Company had a sufficient quantity of tea in their warehouses to supply the demands of the country for two years, during which time the Chinese would have had a more ample and stronger testimony of the value of Bristish commerce to the country than had been previously enforced on their conviction.

The opinion of Mr. Fitzhugh, as given in 1791, has been that invariably pressed on the attention of the Court of Directors by all their supercargoes : " Our trade with China might have been rendered safe and honourable, had not an ill-founded apprehension deterred us from reclaiming those privileges of which we have, by gradual encroachments, been clandestinely deprived." That the Chinese are themselves not altogether blind to the importance of the trade to their own country, may be believed on the evidence of the governor of Canton. Addressing the emperor, he says, " This prosperous dynasty has shewn tenderness and great benevolence to foreigners, and admitted them to a general market, for a hundred and some scores of years, during which time they have traded quietly and peaceably together, without any trouble. How, then, would it suddenly put a barrier before them, and cut off the trade? Besides, in Canton there are several hundreds of thousands of poor unemployed people, who have heretofore obtained their livelihood by trading in foreign merchandise. If in one day they should lose the means of gaining a livelihood, the evil consequences to the place would be great. We, your ministers, who are responsible for giving rest to the people, and shewing favour towards the merchants, ought to unite our powers, and conjointly form plans," &c.

Such a temporary stoppage of trade would bring no loss on the revenue, since the East India Company, having a two years' stock on hand, would continue to supply the market as usual, during such a temporary interruption. The Bengal opium trade, being contraband at all times, need not be affected by the suspension of the British branch of the commerce.

The policy of supporting the insolvent hongs having been adopted by the supercargoes, and sanctioned by the Board of Directors, was for some time opposed by the local government, which even went so far as to obtain an order from the emperor to declare them bankrupts. But a sum equal to 133,000*l.* sterling, as presents to the principal authorities, extracted from the five hongs that were labouring under this predicament, and which amount was advanced by the other merchants under the guarantee of the Company's supercargoes, induced the mandarins to intercede in their behalf. The debts of those five merchants to European creditors, are said to have aggregated nearly a million sterling. Most of them have since failed. The first appears to have been Shy Kin Qua, in 1805 ; Consequa and Ex Chin subsequently; Poonqua died insolvent ; another died on the way to his place of banishment ; young Chung-qua hanged himself ; Pacqua was banished ; Manhop likewise died, on his way to Elee ; Gow-qua was imprisoned for traitorous connection with the English, and died in confinement. Perhaps even this list of hongs, ruined by mandarin extortion, is incomplete. One merchant is still imprisoned on the stale pretext of traitorous connexion with the English, on the ground that Lord Napier came up from Whampoa to Canton in the boats of the Fort William, country ship, for which this man was security.

This is not a case that ought to be passed over without notice. Charge of traitorous connexion with foreigners, implies treasonable conduct on the part of those foreigners, from which they cannot be considered as fully exonerated while any man remains subjected to that charge. It would be but acting conformably to the claims of humanity, as well as of justice and good policy, to require that this unfortunate man be compensated for all his sufferings. Such a step would put an end to the practice hitherto constantly resorted to, of endeavouring to gain any desired points from foreigners by threatening cruelty to those natives for whom they may be supposed to feel an interest.

The case of the linguist, Ayew, was of the same description. This man was employed by the super-cargoes to carry a portrait of the Prince Regent to Pekin. It is also said that he was the carrier of a gold snuff-box and a friendly letter from Mr. Elphinstone, then chief of the factory, to a former governor of Canton, the worthy Ta-Jin Sung, of whom honourable mention is made in Lord Macartney's embassy. Sung, while governor of Canton in 1811, is said to have admitted the chief supercargoes to no fewer than nine conferences in the course of six months; to have given and received entertainments, and otherwise to have evinced great kindness and good feeling towards the English. The dread of a direct communication between the English and the court was probably the motive for seizing Ayew. The charge actually made against this man, and on which he was seized, was treason; but when a spirited remonstrance was made on that subject, and on several others, the mandarins had no hesitation in falsely declaring that there was no such charge preferred against the man, as the emperor himself had made no objection to the receipt of the present by Sung, but that it was a matter which wholly regarded the laws of China, and was nothing more than that he, having been in a menial situation, had endeavoured to purchase rank. An official declaration was even obtained from the viceroy to this effect, though by a copy of his letter to the court of Pekin, privately obtained, there is a direct assertion to the contrary. Such were the tortures inflicted on this poor man, that he endeavoured to destroy himself in prison, by swallowing opium. He was in the end banished, for sixteen years, to Elee.

It is obvious, that with such proofs against them, they must have regarded with great anxiety the contemplated embassy of Lord Amherst in 1816; but the falsehoods regarding the English, which they had reported to Pekin on this very occasion, as well as the manner in which Admiral Drury's visit had been represented, had, no doubt, some weight in prejudicing the emperor's mind against the country and its representative.

As pertinacity has by some been thought a striking feature in Chinese character, and as the steadiness with which consent to the occupation of Macao was refused, is considered as illustrative of that trait, it is of importance to show, that such pertinacity never stands in the way of their interest after the expectation of concessions from their antagonists has ceased. The maxim of a Chinese politician is to make, under all circumstances, the best terms he can. If bullying and circumvention do not produce submission within due time, he next tries how little will satisfy his opponent. Thus, in 1813, when the residence at Canton of Mr. Roberts, who presided over the Company's affairs in 1809, was objected to, on the ostensible ground of his having advanced money on contracts to hong merchants, contrary, as was alleged, (though falsely,) to Chinese law, the viceroy, after three months suspension of trade, was fain to resign the contest, though he had previously, in edict after edict, published his determination to carry the point. The hoppo, who had urged on the governor on this occasion, was said to have privately expressed his belief, that the more violent and arbitrary he showed himself towards foreigners and the hong merchants, the more would he have it in his power to profit by extortion. The firmness of the supercargoes, however, defeated his schemes. He published edicts prohibiting the supercargoes from addressing government on the subject of their grievances, declaring that foreigners are indebted to the clemency of his imperial majesty for their trade, and for permission to tread the ground, and eat the herbs in common with the Chinese; and if after that notice, foreigners presumed of their own accord to make applications to government, the viceroy would, on discovery, request his majesty's permission to punish them severely. Natives were prohibited from serving Europeans, and the factories were suddenly entered into, and all the Chinese attendants seized. A prohibition was published against supplying kings' ships with provisions, and intercourse between them and merchant ships proscribed; while the private boats of merchant ships, contrary to immemorial usage and express stipulations formally entered upon, were seized for want of custom-house passes, though they had no goods on board. It was at this time the arrest, already noticed, of the linguist, Ayew, took place.

The supercargoes prohibited the Company's ships from entering the river. The viceroy began to see he had gone too far, and told the hong merchants he would allow a mandarin to discuss the matter in dispute with Sir George Staunton. Meetings took place on four successive days, when the viceroy suddenly broke off the conferences. Sir George directed all British subjects to leave Canton, and ordered the ships at Whampoa to join the others below the forts. While these measures were in the course of execution, a deputation from Canton brought an invitation to renew the conferences. Sir George returned accordingly, but was immediately informed that the opening of the trade must be preliminary to any further discussion. Sir George saw through the trick, and freely expressing his indignation at such conduct, threatened again to withdraw.

The viceroy finding this artifice fail, mandarins were now sent by him to negotiate in earnest. Every point was conceded, or matters of offence explained away. As already stated, a false gloss was put on the arrest of the linguist; permission to address the government was restored; all intentional contempt, in the application of the terms MAN and EE, positively disavowed. A promise was given that no official visits would in future be paid to the factories, without previous notice of the purport. Boats were to be allowed to pass to and from Whampoa as before. Servants of all descriptions, except some unknown classes named *Shawan* and *Keupan*, might be freely hired. Ships of war were allowed to anchor at their usual stations; and notice was to be given in future when natives were to be tried on charges in which foreigners were implicated. An edict to the foregoing effect was published on the 2d of December, 1814. It was after this successful exhibition of what might be effected by the firmness and judgment of one man, who was master

H

of the language and of the character of the people he
had to do with, that ministers and the court of
directors resolved on sending Lord Amherst on an
embassy to Pekin.

The capricious and vexatious proceedings of which
the supercargoes had complained, had been effectu-
ally checked for the time. To prevent their repetition,
with all the interruption to commerce and loss that
the successful resistance of them required, was no
doubt an object of some importance. The wretched
mistake was to question our right to demand from
the sovereign of the country such a pledge, in the
shape of an express stipulation, against their recur-
rence, as would give our own government the power
of interfering in behalf of its subjects, as often as
injurious measures were pursued against them. The
edict of 1814 was but a compact of the Chinese
government on the one hand, and, on the other,
of individuals who had no means of compelling
the observance of its stipulations, and who, in case
of their being broken, had no remedy; for it would
be the height of folly and imbecility to call that
step a remedy, by the adoption of which their affairs
would be ruined.

It was admitted, even in the milk-and-water sum-
mary of the objects that were proposed for this
embassy, that "if the Chinese government were, in
an unfriendly, inhospitable spirit, by inequitable
conduct to force to a close a pacific intercourse which
has subsisted so long, and in which this country has
embarked so great a capital, it could hardly fail to
resent such a harsh and injurious proceeding."
Such is the one spark of fire which glimmers amid

the mass of dead ashes and rubbish, of which the rest of the document consists. Had his majesty contented himself with a letter to the emperor, stating that he rejoiced at the late adjustment of differences, inasmuch as he had at one time feared that the unfriendly, inhospitable, and inequitable conduct of the local government would have compelled him to put an end to the amicable relations which had previously subsisted between the two countries, his imperial majesty of China would have given the most attentive, if not the most gratified ear to any thing further his Britannic majesty might have to propose, with a view to the maintenance of concord for the future ; while presents, though not tribute, and an ambassador, though not the representative of an imperial vassal, might have found a gracious reception at the imperial throne.

What other language would the ministers of the king of England dare to employ, on his majesty's behalf, if they were addressing another government, in the face of the powers of Europe, under similar circumstances ? Let the secret of their folly and meanness be told : they ignorantly and blindly believed that the commerce of China might be lost if they ceased to cringe, and that, with the tea trade, there would be a loss to the revenue of three millions per annum. Security, not danger, to the trade, would have accrued from such an indication of resolution to support those who were engaged in it. Had it, however, been possible that that expectation would have been disappointed, other nations would have imported tea on terms equally advantageous

H 2

to the country as those obtained from the East India Company, while the revenue would have been collected as easily and as fully as ever.

As to the other objects of the mission, the appointment of a consul at Canton was no object so long as the right of the chief supercargo to address the government was recognised; and there was nothing in the character of the recent intercourse that could have been, by any rational being, considered as marking out the occasion as a fit one for asking admission to other ports.

It would be useless for our present purpose to add to the abundant evidence already afforded, of the insolence and mendacity that form such prominent features of the Chinese public character, by citing further instances from the histories of Lord Amherst's unhappy embassy. Any one who can patiently read what is there narrated, may find examples, taken from the emperor downwards, sufficient to satiate him, *usque ad nauseam.* It is difficult to conceive how an administration that, with all its faults and weaknesses, had so recently given peace to Europe, could have digested the treatment of its ambassador by a nation whose imbecility can only be equalled by the offensiveness of its lofty pretensions. They acted, however, as if they were quite conscious of the favour that had been shown to their minister, when, to use the imperial words, his majesty "sent down his pleasure to expel these ambassadors, and send them back to their own country, without punishing the high crime they had committed."

The Canton government, taking its cue from Pekin, violated its engagements of 1814, refusing to receive addresses from the supercargoes, and imprisoning and maltreating their servants as traitorously attached to the English. Luckily they went a step further, where they could not so easily move with impunity. They fired on his majesty's ship Alceste, at one of the recognised anchorages for ships of war. The insult was returned—the fort silenced—Captain Maxwell proceeded to Canton—demanded an explanation—got a satisfactory reply—and no opposition was made when his majesty's ship Lyra passed the forts, and proceeded to Whampoa.

How was the report of these events received at home? Did the ministry and the Court of Directors see that a barbarous nation must be coerced, if she will not spontaneously comport herself with the good faith and decencies that are necessary in all international dealings? It was enjoined on the supercargoes "to observe the utmost moderation and temper in all discussions with authorities so constituted as those of China" — "however evident it might appear that the authorities at Canton considered themselves at liberty to exercise a conduct so directly contrary to the agreement concluded between the Select Committee and the viceroy and hoppo of Canton, in the year 1814"— and "that the duty of the Select Committee called for the adoption of moderation and forbearance in all their intercourse with the Chinese." "Allowances should be at all times made for the known habits of the Chinese in their official correspondence." Allowance for the known habits of the rapacious tyrant, the false knave, and the cowardly bully, was what the Court were in fact recommending, and they could not have been blind to that fact. But they had got a good thing, and like the Chinese government, wished to conduct it quietly, no matter at what expense of character, but so as to make no noise, lest, in the confusion, their incompetence should be discovered, and it should slip out of their hands.

In a later instance, the East India Directors having occasion to expatiate on the beauty and moral fitness of truth, an evasion of which, (under circumstances that went, as far as possible, to render deception excusable,) had saved their servants the probable necessity of coming to a violent rupture with the Chinese, declared their decided opinion, that the " maintenance of the British character for truth and honour may be considered the key-stone of our influence and well-being in that extraordinary country." Strange that with such a conviction and clear perception of a most important and irrefragable truth, they did not see the falsehood and dishonour of acquiescing in the attribute of " *submissive dependence*," untruly applied to their sovereign, and to the designation of " *barbarians*," untruly applied to their servants ; and that they should have been seemingly unconscious that all that opposed our influence and well-being in that extraordinary country hung upon those false admissions, as an arch from its key-stone.

In direct contradiction of the notion that the Chinese are a people who will have their own way, it would be much more correct to characterize them, as, of all the nations on the earth, the most easily obliged to eat their own words. We

have already given numerous instances of this sort.
We may add the case of the determination of the
viceroy to stop the trade till some victims to his
revenge should be delivered up by Captain Richardson, of the Topaze frigate, some Chinese who
had attacked a watering party of that ship having
been killed in the fray. To this suspension of the
trade, during which " he (the viceroy) would not
permit so much as a thread of silk, or the down of
a plant to be shipped," until the foreign murderers
were delivered up by the supercargoes, in whose
power they were not, he added a threat of making
the supercargoes themselves personally responsible,
if they continued disobedient.

The supercargoes withdrew, ordered their ships
to make the best of their way out, and prevented
new arrivals from entering the river. Captain
Richardson sailed from his anchorage. The viceroy
first withdrew his threat of making the supercargoes personally responsible ; then offered to
renew the trade, if a promise was made that those
whom he called guilty, should be punished in
England ; and ended by a renewal of commercial
intercourse, on the simple condition that a state-
ment of facts should be rendered to the Court of
Directors, in order that the guilt of the offenders
might be inquired into. The viceroy, however, did
not fail to gloss over the inconsistency, by a proclamation full of the most gross misrepresentation and
perversion of facts.

It is only within the last few years, that the
labours of the late Rev. Dr. Morrison have made
us acquainted with passing events in the interior of

China, through the medium of the English periodical press at Canton. During that time there have been five rebellions, in all of which the insurgents have been either bought over, as in the case of the Canton pirates, or taken by treachery, after the imperial troops have sustained the most signal defeats. The Tartar conquest of China was, in fact, a mere march into an unresisting country, or the seizure of opposing chieftains, by stratagem, or through the corruption of their followers.

During the discussions with Lord Napier, their preparations against the expected approach of the boats' crews of two frigates to Canton, were such as, by any other nation, would have been adopted, only under the apprehension of invasion by a powerful army. They made a show of placing troops and guns for the defence of Macao. The Portuguese governor, however, considering their presence as an insult, gave notice to their commander, that if they did not re-embark, he would open his batteries upon them. The officer begged time for reference to his commander-in-chief, which was granted, and as the Portuguese governor showed himself in earnest, his ally did as he was bid. In the viceroy's despatches, the Portuguese barbarians are praised accordingly, as " having manifested, in a high degree, reverential submission, having been roused to express their willingnes to guard themselves."

With a dozen of marines for his personal guard, Lord Napier could not be forced from his house at Canton, by all the expedients that were resorted to for the purpose.

The appearances of Chinese valour, described by
Lindsay and Gutzlaff, are in the highest degree
ludicrous. Landing at Chapo, Mr. Gutzlaff and
two or three other Europeans found an armed force
drawn up along the shore. The soldiers had matchlocks and burning matches ready for a volley. A
Tartar general had placed himself in a temple to
superintend the operations. Being accustomed to
the sight of Chinese batteries, which seldom do
hurt, and knowing that their matchlocks are not
made to hit, they passed the formidable line in
peace. The soldiers retreated, and the crowd. of
people in the rear being very dense, a great part of
the camp was overrun, so that the tents fell to the
ground.

A Chinese admiral having run foul of the ship
Amherst, and then, in spite of all remonstrance, let
go his anchor so close astern that the same accident
was sure to recur on the change of the tide, Mr.
Lindsay sent his launch, with ten men and two
officers, to cut the Junk's cable. " There were no
arms whatever in the boat except two short axes.
The launch arrived alongside at the moment the
Junk let go her second anchor ; and Mr. Simpson,
the second mate, and the gunner, jumped on board
with axes in their hands, followed by Mr. Jauncey
and another man, totally unarmed. On seeing them
come on deck, the Chinese crew, in number forty
or fifty, were seized with such a panic, that one
simultaneous rush was made forward. Some ran
below, some over the bows, several leaped head-
foremost into the water, and the party of four were
left in possession of the deck. The only persons to

be seen on deck, were the admiral and his personal servant, both of whom seemed in the greatest state of alarm."—" This trifling *fracas* was unattended with any unpleasant circumstances, nor did it in the least interrupt the friendly intercourse with the mandarins. On the contrary, it appeared to increase the estimation in which the foreigners were held; and one very satisfactory result was, that from that day, no war junks were anchored within half a mile of the 'Amherst,' excepting when they came to trade."

To prevent the Amherst from entering the *Woo Sung* river, in which stands SHANG HAE, all the military and naval forces of the neighbourhood were put in requisition; tents were erected; and great guns, without carriages, were placed along on each side of the river; and to make the display still more imposing, a row of mud heaps, in the form of tents, were thrown up, and then white-washed; and, finally, fifteen imperial junks stationed themselves in the mouth of the river. But the "Lord Amherst" contemptuously passed between those formidable lines, and anchored some way up the river. Neither threats nor entreaties prevailed with the barbarians to swerve from their course. In more than one instance did the imperial officers prostrate themselves, and offer to perform the *Ko-tow*. Similar examples, without number, of the pusillanimity of the Chinese, in a military point of view, might be instanced, and some from the writer's personal observation. These are not alluded to with a view of inciting to an attempt to conquest or unjust aggression of any sort, but to show how little room there is to apprehend that, in the performance of

the duty imposed on our country of vindicating her
insulted dignity, resort to actual hostilities will be
necessary. There is not, in the history of the last
two hundred years, a single instance in which
European troops have been attacked by Chinese,
however great the disparity of numbers.

This difficulty removed, the next is that of over-
coming the aversion of the emperor to compromise
his "respect," by yielding to the dictation of
foreigners. We might, perhaps, safely leave it to
Chinese ingenuity to discover a loop-hole by which
that knot may be disentangled; but it is well to
leave a bridge for the escape of a timid enemy.
There can be no doubt that Governor Loo has, in
fact, grossly misrepresented all that occurred between
himself and the late Lord Napier; and we have a right
to take it for granted that, had the state of circumstances been made known to the emperor, Loo would
have been severely punished, and another person
appointed in his room, with instructions to receive the
king of England's commissioner with due respect.
It must also be assumed, that his imperial majesty
is unaware of the contemptuous manner in which his
royal brother is commonly mentioned by his public
officers; and equally so of the studied indignities
heaped on his subjects. Common justice can be
granted without any lowering of respect, even though
the claim should be made by an envoy with an army
and fleet as his escort; nor even though the imperial
courtiers should screen the light of truth from his
eyes till the arrival of the British envoy extraordinary with a few thousand followers at Pekin,
will it then be too late for him to perceive how

grossly he has been deceived, and how worthy Englishmen are of being cherished even as the people of China. It is possible, indeed, that until the interpreter of the British envoy shall be able to explain matters in person, they may not be fully developed to his majesty's sublime apprehension; but a single audience cannot fail to make all things clear as day. Of course, till they are so, and have been made equally manifest to the whole empire through approved edicts published in the Pekin Gazette, and the consequences deducible therefrom admitted under seal and signature, our envoy with his escort must be precluded from re-embarking.

The following may be taken as a rough sketch of the admissions required; and it will be found that it contains nothing incompatible with the honour or interests of China, unless bare compensation for injury can, by any possibility, be so considered.

OBJECTS OF THE EXPEDITION OR MISSION.

1st. *To obtain a recognition of the King of England as the independent sovereign of a civilized country.*

    A. As such his style is " WHANG TE."

    B. His address, " Elder Brother," mutually with the Emperor of China.

    C. English people must no longer be called EE, or MAN-EE, but *Ying Le Jin,* " Men of the English nation."

D. They must no longer be treated as MAN-EE, (barbarians) but must have the same right to protection from wrongs as natives.

E. They must not, therefore, be *placed under the control of native merchants*, but must be answerable to the regular tribunals, each for his own acts.

F. Natives must not be held responsible to the government for the conduct of Englishmen.

G. Natives must not be excited to treat Englishmen with aversion or contempt, by any proclamation stigmatising them as prone to vice, or denying to them any privilege enjoyed by natives. Thus, all cause of disturbances will be avoided, as far as these arise from the insults which foolish, idle, and mischievous people have hitherto been led to think they can offer, with impunity, to any foreigner.

H. Englishmen may freely inquire, what articles of foreign produce, or manufacture, would be acceptable to the people of China. They may ascertain what prices could be obtained for such articles, in order that they may know whether they can afford to import them into China at those rates. No native shall be liable to punishment for affording, or procuring for them, such information.

I. They may freely inquire what articles of produce or manufacture are procurable in the various provinces of China, and at what prices, that they may know which of them will suit the foreign market. No native shall be liable to punishment for giving, or procuring, such information. By the adoption of these two rules, the poor of China may be supplied with warm and cheap clothing in return for the produce of their skill and labour; while the rich may be able to procure greater comforts from the expenditure of their money; whereas, by the keeping prices secret, all consumers are obliged to pay extravagant prices, to the enrichment of useless middle men at their expense, and are unable to obtain fair value either for their own money, or for their goods.

2nd. *To require an apology for the treatment of Lord Napier*, as* COMMISSIONER *of the* KING OF ENGLAND.

    A. As such, Lord Napier was a KIN CHAE, who, according to Chinese rules of eti-

---

* It is generally believed, that during the late struggle of Lord Napier, the hong merchants were encouraged to recommend to the mandarins, that they should persevere in refusing to receive his lordship's communications to the viceroy, and in requiring his immediate departure from Canton, by the approving opinions imprudently expressed to them *by an English resident of some influence* at the place. The report may not be correct, but it is countenanced by several of the facts of the case, and it will be right to guard against such an occurrence in future.

quette, takes precedence of all other
official ranks, governors of provinces
included. None but independent sovereigns, holding imperial sway, can use
the word KIN, in its application to their
envoys or commissioners, but, *e converso*,
all sovereigns of independent empires
signify that independence by the use of
that word. There is none higher; therefore, none other admissible on the part of
the sovereign of the British empire.

B. As KIN CHAE of an independent sovereign,
not inferior in any respect to the sovereign of China, no viceroy *can* refuse to
correspond, and to inter-visit, with the
English commissioner.

C. No mandarin of inferior rank, far less hong
merchants, can be interposed as a medium of communication; while, on the
contrary, it will be the duty of the hoppo
to wait on the commissioner when any
matter regarding trade is to be discussed.

D. So also the *Gan-Cha-Sze* must wait on the
commissioner when any matter relative
to criminal justice, as regards Englishmen, is under deliberation.

E. So likewise the *Nan haee Heen* on subjects
of police.

3rd. *Compensation must be made for the losses caused
to British merchants by the stoppage of the trade*

while Lord Napier was at Canton, and for some time
after his departure.

A. The trade must not in future be stopped,
without giving merchants sufficient warn-
ing, so that no more ships may be
sent out from England, on the faith of its
continuance, and that the cargoes already
arrived, and on their way, may be disposed of, and their value realized.

B. No new imposts, burthens, or impediments,
of any kind, must be laid on commerce,
without similar notice, — say, of at the
least, eighteen months.

C. The trade shall not be at any time stopped
capriciously, or for any reasons incompatible with a friendly feeling towards
the British nation

D. If such a measure be adopted with a view
of inflicting an injury on the English
nation, it must, of course, be considered
as an act of hostility.

E. To prevent the danger of misunderstanding,
it will therefore be necessary, that the
motives which really induce the emperor
of China to put an end to the commerce
of Englishmen in his country, be com-
municated to the English commissioner,
for the satisfaction of his government.

F. Also, when the government of China shall
stop the trade of any individual British
subject, or expel him altogether from the
country, the commissioner shall be in-

formed of the reasons of such treatment, and of the measures taken for the security of any property that may be in the hands of such British subject.

4th. *Until particular rules are framed by the consent of both governments, British subjects shall not, for any wrong done either to another British subject, or to a Chinese subject, be liable to more severe punishment than is applicable to the like offence by the laws of England.*

A. That the nature of the offence may be fully understood, and the laws applicable thereto properly known, it is necessary that, in every case in which a British subject is implicated in a court of justice, the. British commissioner, or some one appointed by him for that purpose, shall attend during the whole of the trial, so that he may have an opportunity of hearing every tittle of the evidence.

B. He must have a linguist to explain to him each word that passes, so that he may write it down; and he may employ a Chinese writer to take the evidence for future reference.

c. No one shall be prevented from explaining to the accused all that passes; or from expressing in the Chinese language any thing he may wish to say.

D. Torture being contrary to the British law, must not, in any shape or degree, be

I

resorted to, where a British subject is implicated.

E. After the whole of the evidence against a British subject has been closed, he shall be at liberty to offer any remarks upon it, and any explanations of his own conduct; and shall also be at liberty to claim the attendance of any witnesses he may think proper to call, and examine them accordingly. His defence may be in writing.

F. On occasions on which the judge may think proper to make a reference to any higher authority whatever, regarding a matter in which a British subject is implicated, a true copy of such reference, or proposed reference, shall be submitted to the British commissioner, that he may accompany it with such remarks as he may deem necessary.

G. So also, when such a case is referred, by any authority whatever, to the Criminal Board at Pekin, or to the emperor.

H. Where British subjects have not rendered themselves amenable to the laws, their acts shall not be visited with punishment on the natives they have employed, or who have been joined with them in their lawful acts.

I. On the death of any British subject, having no legal representative on the spot, the Chinese authorities shall give over charge of his property to the British commis-

sioner, or any other person by him
appointed.

K. No British subject shall be called upon to
conform to any ceremony or practice
inconsistent with the religion he pro-
fesses, and with the usages, in like cases,
of his country.

L. All British subjects shall be at entire liberty
to observe, without molestation, their own
civil and religious usages, when these may
be followed without any injury to the
people of China.

5th. *No hoppo, or other authority whatever, shall be
at liberty to impose any tax, or duty, direct or
indirect, on any foreign ships or vessels, on any
articles of export or import, or any boats, coolies, or
other conveyance of goods, other than, or different
from, the prescribed imperial tariff.*

A. The consoo fund must be abolished.

B. The tariff must be rendered simple, clear,
and intelligible, so that no merchant can
doubt the amount of duty to which his
goods are liable.

C. In cases of new articles, not before rated,
they shall be valued by the hoppo, and
pay, according to that valuation, the same
rate of per centage duty as that to which
other goods most nearly resembling them
are liable.

D. In case of dispute, the merchant may require
the hoppo to take the article in question

at his own valuation, with an addition of 12 per cent. for the profit of the importer.

E. If any public officer whatever, or any person pretending to be a public officer, shall ask or accept a fee, not publicly authorised, or any present or exaction whatever from any British subject, or from persons in the employ of, or dealing with a British subject, shall offer any impediment to free and open dealing, the commissioner shall be at liberty to represent such extortion or hindrance, however disguised, to the proper authority, that redress may be afforded, and the wrongdoer punished according to the laws of the country.

F. If, from any principle of policy, the Chinese government should altogether prohibit, or place so high a duty on any article as to tempt British subjects to smuggling, the law of China may be freely applied to its suppression, without the assistance of the British authority; it being the duty of every government to carry into effect its own revenue laws, although it is not incumbent on other governments to assist her in so doing, to the prejudice of their own subjects.

G. As silver is silver in whatever shape it may be cast, its relative value in each form depends entirely on its quantity and fineness, with which the natives of China are fully as familiar as those of England ; there shall therefore be no prohibition from dealing in silver in any shape that may best suit the convenience of the parties.

II. To prevent general smuggling, goods, after being weighed and numbered on board ship by the hoppo's officers, shall be delivered into the custody of the hoppo, in warehouses of his own ; the hoppo giving at the same time an acknowledgment of their receipt. On payment of the duties, the goods shall be delivered in the same perfect state and condition to the order of the party to whom receipts have been granted; the hoppo being answerable for any loss or damage sustained by the fault or negligence of his people, or the insufficiency of warehouses, or by fire, or theft.

6th. *Vessels not engaged in trade shall pay the ordinary pilotage, but no other duty or charge whatever. They shall be freely allowed to purchase refreshments and articles requisite for repair or refit, and to hire workmen for such purpose.*

A. No fee, or tax of any kind, shall be required from the people dealing with, or employed by, such ships.

7th. *Merchant vessels shall pay shipping charges of all kinds, according to their real size, as ascertained by their certificate of registry. None of the persons engaged in supplying them with provisions, or stores, shall be subject to any fee or exaction whatever in that capacity.*

A. The cumsha, which was originally an authorised exaction for the private benefit of
the hoppo, is a heavy addition to the tax
paid by native vessels. Let a tax on
goods be substituted for it ; but, in the
meantime, let it be graduated according to
measurement. It is bad policy to continue the present high charges on small
ships, because it induces them to evade
all charges by not coming into harbour at
all, and to carry on illicit trade outside.

B. Commanders of vessels shall be at perfect
liberty to engage their own compradores
and linguists, on such terms as may be
mutually agreed upon.

C. In case of the fraudulent, or other improper
conduct of compradores, their employers
shall have immediate redress from a
Chinese officer, whose station may be in
the neighbourhood of the shipping, inasmuch as justice would be defeated by
the smallest delay when ships are on the
eve of departure.

8th. *British subjects may take their families to any
place where they reside themselves, and may employ
any sort of vehicle they may find agreeable or convenient, as freely as natives.*

A. When the sumptuary laws of China pre-
scribe certain equipages for particular

ranks, they must be conformed to by British subjects. It will be the duty of the commissioner to examine the pretensions of each individual, and to certify the class of equipage that his rank may entitle him to maintain.

9th. *British subjects may visit any part of the country under passports signed by the British commissioner, and countersigned by the Chinese authority at the place.*

A. Such travelling passports must, of course, specify the place to which the traveller is desirous of proceeding, and the time required for his journey. Should further time become necessary, such extension must be granted, and noted, by the chief authority of the place in which it is applied for.

10th. *A British subject desirous of residing for a lawful object in any part of the country, shall report himself in person to the chief magistrate of the place, specifying his lodging, and shall do the same as often as he may change his lodging; but shall not thereafter be in any way molested or controlled in his pursuits, so long as they are conducted in a lawful and inoffensive manner.*

11th. *British ships may proceed to any port in China at which an imperial custom-house has been established, and land and ship goods as freely, and on the same terms, as at Canton. Should there be no*

British commissioner or deputy commissioner at such port, British subjects that may be charged with any offences must be sent for trial to the nearest port at which a British commissioner resides.

12th. *British traders may have boats, or other conveyance, to carry goods from any one port of the country to another, paying the same rates of transit duties as natives.*

After what has been stated, there is little required to show the justice and necessity of those articles, if we desire to carry on a commercial intercourse with China, on a footing consistent with honour, security, and advantage, national and individual. Those are the prizes : it rests with the voice of the country to determine whether the present glorious opportunity for their attainment shall be availed of, or whether, like so many others that have preceded it, it shall, to the injury alike of China and of England, be permitted to pass unimproved ; leaving the British name and British interests to sink still lower in the scale of degradation than the point to which short-sighted avarice and imbecility have already reduced them.

APPENDIX.

KING'S MOST EXCELLENT MAJESTY

IN COUNCIL.

*The Petition of the undermentioned British Subjects
at Canton.*

HUMBLY SHEWETH,

That we are induced, by the extra-ordinary position in which we feel ourselves placed in relation to the Chinese government, to petition your Majesty in Council to take such measures as may be adapted alike to maintain the honour of our country, and the advantages which a safe and uninterrupted commerce with China is calculated to yield to the revenues of Great Britain, and to the important classes interested in its arts and manufactures.

The extraordinary state of our relations with the Chinese induces us to petition your Majesty.

We beg humbly to represent, that at the present moment, the Commissioners appointed by your Majesty to superintend the affairs of British subjects trading at Canton, are not acknowledged by the constituted authorities of this country, and that they are not permitted to reside within the limits to which their jurisdiction is, by their commission, strictly confined ; while they are forbidden by their instructions to appeal to the imperial government at Peking, and are perfectly powerless to resent the indignities offered to the late chief superintendent, or to compel reparation for the injuries done to your Majesty's subjects by the late unprovoked stoppage of their trade.

Your Majesty's superintendents are prohibited by the Chinese from exercising their functions : and are not empowered by your Majesty to appeal to Peking.

Your petitioners are well persuaded that the powers vested in your Majesty's commissioners were thus restricted with the express object of avoiding, as far as possible, all occasion of collision with the Chinese authorities; while it was hoped that, by maintaining a direct intercourse with the principal officers of government, instead of indirectly communicating through the hong merchants, a sure way would be opened for the improvement of the present very objectionable footing on which foreign merchants stand in this country, and for security against the many wrongs and inconveniences which they have had to suffer in the present state of their commercial avocations.

The whole history of intercourse with China proves that the most unsafe of all courses in treating with its government is that of submission to contempt or wrongs.

Your petitioners, however, beg leave most earnestly to submit to your Majesty in council, their thorough conviction, founded on the invariable tenor of the whole history of foreign intercourse with China, as well as of its policy on occasions of internal commotion, down to the present moment, that the most unsafe of all courses that can be followed in treating with the Chinese government, or any of its functionaries, is that of quiet submission to insult, or such unresisting endurance of contemptuous or wrongful treatment, as may compromise the honour, or bring into question the power of our country. We cannot, therefore, but deeply deplore that such authority to negotiate, and such force to protect from insult, as the occasion demands, were not entrusted to your Majesty's commissioners, confident as we are, without a shadow of doubt,

If Lord Napier had been furnished with force and authority to resent insult, we are confident, without a shadow of doubt, that his mission would have succeeded.

that, had the requisite powers, properly sustained by an armed force, been possessed by your Majesty's late first commissioner, the lamented Lord Napier, we should not now have to deplore the degraded and insecure position in which we are placed, in consequence of the representative of our Sovereign having been compelled to retire from Canton without having authority to offer any remonstrance to the supreme government, or to make a demonstration of a resolution to obtain reparation at once, for the insults wantonly heaped upon him by the local authorities.

We pray your Majesty to grant powers plenipotentiary to an officer of diplomatic

Your petitioners, therefore, humbly pray that your Majesty will be pleased to grant powers plenipotentiary to such person of suitable rank, discretion, and diplomatic experience, as your Majesty, in your wisdom may think fit and proper to be entrusted with such authority; and your petitioners would suggest that he be directed to proceed to a convenient station on the east coast of China, as near to the capital of the country as may be found most expedient, in one of your Majesty's ships of the line, attended by a sufficient maritime force, which we are of opinion need not consist of more than two frigates, and three or four armed vessels of light draft, together with a steam vessel, all fully manned; that he may, previously to landing, require, in the first instance, in the name of your Majesty, ample reparation for the insults offered by the governor of Kwangtung and Kwangse in his edicts published on the occasion of Lord Napier's arrival at Canton, and the subsequent humiliating conduct pursued towards his Lordship, to which the aggravation of his illness and death may be attributed; as well as for the arrogant and degrading language used towards your Majesty and our country in edicts emanating from the local authorities, wherein your Majesty was represented as the "reverently submissive" tributary of the Emperor of China, and your Majesty's subjects as profligate barbarians, and that they be retracted, and never again employed by Chinese functionaries: that he may also demand reparation for the insult offered to your Majesty's flag by firing on your Majesty's ships of war from the forts at the Bogue, and that remuneration shall be made to your Majesty's subjects for the losses they have sustained by the detention of their ships during the stoppage of their trade. After these preliminaries shall have been conceded (as your petitioners have no doubt they will be), and not till then, your petitioners humbly suggest that it will be expedient for your Majesty's plenipotentiary to propose the appointment of commissioners on the part of the Chinese government, to adjust with him, on shore, such measures as may be deemed most effectual to the prevention of future occasion of complaint and misunderstanding, and for the promotion and extension of the trade generally, to the mutual advantage of both coun-

Marginal notes:

experience to proceed to China in a ship of the line, with two frigates, sloops, and a steamer;

to require reparation for insults and wrongs to Lord Napier, terminating in that nobleman's death; for firing on your Majesty's ships, and for offensive edicts representing your Majesty as a "reverently submissive" tributary, and your subjects as profligate barbarians; also remuneration for losses arising from stoppage of trade:

thereafter to propose mutually beneficial arrangements; in agreeing to which we do not anticipate difficulty,

124

tries. Your petitioners believe, that if these matters shall be fairly represented, so as to do away with all reasonable objection, and the favourable inclination of the Chinese commissioners be gained, there will be found little disposition on the part of the supreme government to withhold its assent, and every desirable object will thus have been attained.

nor risk of interruption to the Canton trade,

Your petitioners would humbly entreat your Majesty's favourable view of these suggestions, in the confidence that they may be acted upon, not only with every prospect of success, but without the slightest danger to the existing commercial intercourse,

as the force recommended would enable the plenipotentiary to secure indemnity for wrongs by reprisals on the Chinese trade, and by intercepting the imperial revenues in transitu; should such measures be necessary;

inasmuch, as even with a force not exceeding that which we have proposed should be placed at the disposal of your Majesty's plenipotentiary, there would be no difficulty, should proceedings of a compulsory nature be required, in putting a stop to the greater part of the external and internal commerce of the Chinese empire;—in intercepting its revenues in their progress to the capital, and in taking possession of all the armed vessels of the country. Such measures would not only be sufficient to evince both the power and spirit of Great Britain to resent insult, but would enable your Majesty's plenipotentiary to secure indemnity for any injury that might, in the first instance, be offered to the persons or property of your Majesty's subjects; and would speedily induce the Chinese government to submit to just and reasonable terms. We are, at the same time, confident that resort even

which we anxiously wish to avoid.

to such measures as these, so far from being likely to lead to more serious warfare, an issue which both our interests and inclinations alike prompt us to deprecate, would be the surest course for avoiding the danger of such a collision.

Re-admission to the ports formerly open, Amoy, &c., would be beneficial in reviving competition.

Your petitioners beg to submit that the mere restoration of the liberty once possessed of trading to Amoy, Ningpo, and Chusan, would be followed by the most beneficial consequences, not merely in the more extended field thereby opened for commercial enterprise, but in the rivalry which would be excited as formerly, in the officers of government at these several ports, to attract the resort of foreign merchants, and thus extend their own opportunities of acquiring emoluments from the trade.

With respect, however, to this point, or any other of commercial interest that it would be expedient to make the subject of negotiation, your petitioners would humbly suggest that your Majesty's minister in China should be instructed to put himself in communication with the merchants of Canton, qualified, as they must be in a certain degree by their experience and observation, to point out in what respect the benefits that might be reaped under a well-regulated system of commercial intercourse, are curtailed or lost in consequence of the restrictions to which the trade is at present subjected, and the arbitrary and irregular exactions to which it is exposed either directly, or not less severely because indirectly, through the medium of the very limited number of merchants licensed to deal with foreigners. As an instance of the latter, your petitioners may state the fact, that the whole expense of the immense preparations lately made by the local government to oppose the expected advance towards Canton of your Majesty's frigates after they had passed the Bogue, has been extorted from the hong merchants ; and as but a few of them are in a really solvent state, they have no other means of meeting this demand, but by combining to tax both the import and export trade.

On all points of commercial grievance, it will be desirable that the plenipotentiary apply for information to the British merchants at Canton.

We would further humbly, but urgently, submit, that as we cannot but trace the disabilities and restrictions under which our commerce now labours, to a long acquiescence in the arrogant assumption of supremacy over the monarchs and people of other countries, claimed by the Emperor of China for himself and his subjects, we are forced to conclude that no essentially beneficial result can be expected to arise out of negotiations in which such pretensions are not decidedly repelled. We most seriously apprehend, indeed, that the least concession or waving of this point under present circumstances, could not fail to leave us as much as ever subject to a repetition of the injuries of which we have now to complain.

To acquiescence in the supremacy claimed by the Chinese over other nations, we trace existing disabilities ; nor while this continues do we think relief attainable.

We pray that your Majesty will not make any concession on this point, preferring, as we do, that your Majesty, rather than acknowledge Chinese supremacy, should leave us to our own resources.

We would, therefore, humbly beseech your Majesty not to be induced by a paternal regard for your subjects trading to this remote empire, to leave it to the discretion of any future representative of your Majesty, as was permitted in the case of the embassy of Lord Amherst, to swerve in the smallest degree from a direct course of calm and dispassionate, but determined maintenance of the true rank of your Majesty's empire in the scale of nations, well assured as we feel, that any descent from such just position, would be attended with worse consequences than if past events were to remain unnoticed, and we were to be left for the future to conduct our concerns with the Chinese functionaries, each as he best may.

We pray that no persons who have been engaged here in trade, or who have submitted to indignities from the Chinese, be employed to negotiate;

It would ill become your Majesty's petitioners to point to any individual as more competent than another to undertake the office of placing on a secure and advantageous footing our commercial relations with this country. We may, however, perhaps be permitted to suggest the inexpediency of assigning such a task to any person previously known in China as connected with commerce conducted under the trammels and degradations to which it has hitherto been subjected, or to any one, in short, who has had the misfortune either in a public or private capacity, to endure insult or injury from Chinese authorities.

that only functionaries accredited from Peking be negotiated with, not those of Canton, and that no British commissioner shall land till assured of a becoming reception.

Equally inexpedient would it be, as appears to your petitioners, to treat with any functionary not specially nominated by the Imperial cabinet, and not on any account with those of Canton, whose constant course of corrupt and oppressive conduct forms a prominent ground of complaint; or to permit any future commissioner to set his foot on the shores of China, until ample assurance is afforded of a reception and treatment suitable to the dignity of a minister of your Majesty, and the honour of an empire that acknowledges no superior on earth.

And your petitioners shall ever pray, &c.

Canton, 9th December, 1834.

W. Jardine	P. F. Robertson
J. Matheson	W. Blenkin
T. Fox	W. S. Boyd

A. Johnstone

A. S. Keating

J. Innes

J. Hamilton

R. Browne

R. Turner

A. Matheson

R. Thom

H. Wright

J. W. Smith

F. Macqueen

J. M'A. Gladstone

J. Lenox

D. Webster

J. B. Compton

J. Slade

J. Watson

C. S. Compton

T. Collingwood

A. Jardine

D. Wilson

W. Allen

J. L. Templer

J. Kellaway

H. Grant

B. Wise

J. Blyth

A. Nairne

T. Larkins

R. Lungley

J. Rees

F. P. Alleyn

H. J. Wolfe

C. R. Read

J. Lobban

W. E. Farrer

A. Stirling

D. R. Caldwell

J. Ainsley

J. Dalrymple

S. Hyde

H. D. Dalrymple

J. K. Jolly

H. Hale

E. Parry

J. T. Lancaster

A. J. Macfarlane

R. Swan

T. Robson

J. Wilson

R. Ferandes

J. Burnett

G. Kennedy

F. Jauncey

J. Middleton

R. L. Fraser

T. Baker

J. Pearson

J. H. Wellbourne

F. Kiernan

W. Fallowfield

R. F. Lewis

J. Robertson

C. Markwick

J. W. Rose

J. W. Graham

W. Haylett

W. M'Killigin

J. Goddard

L. Just, Jr.

J. Lyon

J. L. Wilson

J. P. Griffiths

J. Baker

D. Brown

J. Purdie

T. Wellbank

G. Coombe

E. Routh

&c. &c.

LONDON :
PRINTFD BY STEWART AND CO.,
OLD BAILEY.

www.ingramcontent.com/pod-product-compliance
Ingram Content Group UK Ltd.
Pitfield, Milton Keynes, MK11 3LW, UK
UKHW042151280225
455719UK00001B/270